DOMESDAY BOOK:
A GUIDE

DOMESDAY BOOK
A Guide

R. WELLDON FINN

PHILLIMORE

1973
Published by
PHILLIMORE & CO. LTD.
London and Chichester

Head Office: Shopwyke Hall,
Chichester, Sussex, England

ISBN 0 85033 101 3

Printed in Great Britain by Eyre and Spottiswoode Ltd,
Her Majesty's Printers, at Grosvenor Press, Portsmouth

To the memory of

Sir John Clapham
Professor of Economic History
in the University of Cambridge

who told an undergraduate
'I think the study of Domesday Book would interest you'

and of
John Horace Round

who told him that
to do this faithfully would take him thirty years.

Both were right

PUBLISHER'S NOTE

Since this book went into production Rex Welldon Finn has died. It is perhaps fitting that such an expert on Domesday Book, having devoted a large part of his life to its study, should have written this guide as his last book. Many scholars have derived great benefit from his published works on Domesday Book and it is hoped that many more in the future will be encouraged by this guide to explore 'our earliest public record'.

CONTENTS

page

1 The Background to Domesday Book 1

2 The Inquest 5
The circuits — shire and Hundred-juries — the vill — the manor — provision of the statistics — work of the Inquest — evidence of the juries — distribution of English land to the newcomers

3 The Making of Domesday Book 17
The Exeter Domesday — the Exchequer Domesday — the indexes — the eastern counties volume — *invasiones* and *clamores* — the Summaries — the geld accounts

4 The King's Geld 25
The hide and its divisions — apportionment of hides and carucates — decimal and duodecimal systems — immunities and exemptions — demesne land

5 The Ploughland and the Plough-team 30
The ploughlands formulae — artificialities of estimates — discrepancies between numbers of ploughlands and plough-teams — co-operative tillage

6 The Slaves and the Peasantry 33
Difficulties of estimating population — the slaves — *coliberti* and *buri* — distribution of slaves — *bovarii* — coscets, cottars, and bordars — villeins — duties and holdings of villeins — peasant rents

7 The Free Peasantry and the Lower Middle Classes . . 40
Miscellaneous categories — radmen — Welshmen — *milites* — forms of tenure — commendation — thegnland — free men and sokemen — teams of free men and sokemen — decrease in their numbers — sokeright

8 The Tenants-in-chief 48
Principles of tenure — the lands of the king and his half-brothers — the lands of the Church — the lay barons — castleries — the sub-tenants — the survivors

9 The Land of the Manor 54
Measurements — woodland — pasture — marsh — moorland — meadow — vineyards — extractive industries

10 Other Manorial Equipment 60
Mills — mill values — fisheries — eel-renders — salmon-renders — saltworks and their renders — the wiches — honey-renders — ferries and tolls

ix

A*

11   Farm Animals 65
      Sheep — swine — goats — cows — horses — changes in
      quantities on the demesnes
12   Churches 68
      Absence of full information about churches and priests —
      glebe land — revenues, tithes, and churchscot
13   The Forests 71
      Royal and other forests — parks — foresters — the New Forest
14   Waste Land 74
      Causes of waste — possibility that 'waste' is not the same as
      'totally deserted' — transference of men and equipment from
      wasted vills — waste in and near Wales — valuation of waste
      land
15   The Valuations of Manors 77
      Basis of valuations — rents from the farming of manors — food
      farms — debased coinage — artificial valuations — factors in
      estimations of values — falls and increases in values — the
      obligations of the shires — sundry dues
16   The Towns 88
      Variations in the description of the cities and boroughs —
      urban population figures — the rural element in the boroughs
      — poverty in some towns — new boroughs — castles and
      castleries — markets — mints — burghal obligations — legal
      information — military service — liability for geld — evidence
      given by townsmen
17   After Domesday 99
      The copying of the Inquest proceedings for special purposes —
      early medieval use of Domesday Book — abbreviated copies —
      the commentators
      Short bibliography 102
      Index 104

DOMESDAY BOOK is our earliest public record, and notable testimony to Norman drive and a sound English administration which enabled the Inquest which produced it to do its work so comprehensively and well.

For the amateur it is a most deceptive document, but amateurs may take comfort from the fact that it has frequently deceived professionals also. A cursory glance down a column of text might suggest that except for the place- and proper names and the figures of the statistics all entries are similarly composed. Nothing could be further from the truth. Some shires include information altogether absent from the record for others; in some certain topics appear only intermittently. The composition of some manors is fairly fully indicated, while for most we are given nothing beyond the name of the place by which the manor was known. In an age when few could read and write and still fewer were interested in orthographical accuracy, the strangest perversions of place- and proper names and technical terms became inscribed. Stray items of information appear, and we are left wondering whether they might be of general application or are altogether exotic.

It is a national heritage frequently misused. It is common for topographical writers or estate agents to state that a place is 'mentioned in Domesday Book', as though this was highly unusual. Well over 13,000 towns and villages and hamlets can claim this distinction, while in their enthusiasm they are apt to credit the record with noting heronries and memorial crosses and aged oaks, none of which appears anywhere in the text.

Folio references are here given only where it is thought they might be of service. For the Exchequer text recto and verso of a leaf are indicated by a and b, and i or ii denote the column of the text. References to the volume concerned with the eastern counties are prefaced II; and those to the Exeter Domesday are italicised. Unless it is specifically stated that an item of information is unique, the textual references usually indicate typical entries illustrative of the point under discussion, and in many instances have in consequence been quite arbitrarily selected, or chosen because of their peculiar emphasis. Alternatives could readily have been found.

R.W.F.

Frinton-on-Sea
Feast of St Augustine of Canterbury, 1971

LIST OF ABBREVIATIONS

Abp.   Archbishop.
Acct.   administrator's account.
Admon.   administration bond
Admon. act   administration act
Afft.   affidavit
Alex.   Alexander
als.   alias
And.   Andrew
bach.   bachelor
bart.   baronet
Berks. archd.   Berkshire archdeaconry
bk.   book
bur.   buried
Cath.   Catherine
Cert. of grant of admon.   certificate of grant of administration
Cert. of poverty   certificate of poverty
Chris.   Christopher
Citn.   citation
clk.   clerk
com.   commission
Ct. act.   court act
Ct. ppr.   court paper
d.   dated
Depn.   deposition
Dthy.   Dorothy
E.   east
Edm.   Edmund
Edw.   Edward
Eliz.   Elizabeth
end.   endorsed
esq.   esquire
Exc.   excommunication
exhib.   exhibited
exor.   executor
f.   father
gent.   gentleman
Geo.   George
Gt.   Great
haberdr.   haberdasher
husb.   husbandman
Hy.   Henry
Inv.   inventory
Jas.   James
Jn.   John

Jos. Joseph
jun. junior
Kath. Katherine
kt. knight
Letters of admon. letters of administration
Mart. Martin
Memo. memorandum
Mgt. Margaret
Mich. Michael
Mon. monition
N. north
Nath. Nathaniel
Nich. Nicholas
P.C.C. Prerogative Court of Canterbury
Prob. act probate act
prof. professor
Rct. receipt
Rd., Richard
Renun. renunciation
Revoc. of cav. revocation of caveat
Revoc. of renun. revocation of renunciation
Robt. Robert
S. South
s. son
Sam. Samuel
Sarum court of the Bishop of Salisbury
sen. senior
sis. sister
spin. spinster
swn. sworn
Thos. Thomas
Tn. act tuition act
Tn. bond tuition bond
W. will or west
w. wife
Warrant for admon. warrant for administration
wid. widow or widower
Wm. William
yeo. yeoman

THE BACKGROUND TO DOMESDAY BOOK

NO SURVIVING DOCUMENT tells us just why what has become known as Domesday Book was made. The *Anglo-Saxon Chronicle* merely says that in 1085 'at midwinter the king was at Gloucester with his counsellors . . . and held very deep speech with his wise men about the land, how it was held, and with what men'. A treatise written nearly a hundred years later states that 'William the Conqueror decided . . . to place the government of the conquered on a written basis . . . he sent men of proved discretion on circuit throughout the kingdom. A careful description of the whole country was made by these men . . . this was gathered into a book'.

The king and his advisers had good reasons for investigating conditions in their new acquisition. Earlier in the year it had been necessary to billet a host of mercenary troops imported in consequence of the danger of invasion from Denmark, and this must have demonstrated how little the central authorities knew about the country's resources. Secondly, written information was available in only insufficient volume. Moreover, though a conquered land had been shared out between the royal adherents in accordance with a scheme devised by the king and his advisers, it was known that many estates had not been lawfully acquired, and that much land was being held by no good title. The solution to the problems which presented themselves was to establish the facts by means of sworn evidence, as unprejudiced as could be obtained, and from which there could be no appeal, and then to commit them to writing. Though it has often been suggested that Domesday Book was intended to be a tax register, and does indeed include much concerning liabilities to taxation, it would have been perfectly possible to reckon the tax due, and to increase liabilities where these were unnecessarily small, without creating the elaborate machinery of the Domesday Inquest.

The instructions given to those who conducted the Inquest have not survived. There exists, however, a 12th-century document which includes much of what must have been their terms of reference, prefacing a copy of an account of the lands of Ely Abbey in six counties.

> Here follows the inquisition regarding lands made by the king's barons, that is, by the oath of the sheriff and of all the barons and of all their Frenchmen and of the whole Hundred, of the priest, the reeve, six villeins of each village. That is to say, what is the name of the manor, who held it in the time of King Edward, who holds it now, how many hides are there, how many plough-teams in demesne and how many are held by the tenants, how many villeins, how many cottars, how many slaves, how many freemen, how many sokemen, how much wood, how much meadow, how much pasture, how many mills, how many fisheries, how much has been added or taken away, how much the whole was worth then and how much now, how much each freeman or sokeman had there or has. All this three times, namely, in the time of King Edward, and when King William gave it, and as it is today, and if it is possible that more can be obtained how it is to be obtained.

The *Anglo-Saxon Chronicle* simply says that 'the king caused them to write down . . . how much each man that was settled on the land in England held in land and cattle, and how much it was worth', and goes on to complain 'how narrowly the survey was made'. Another account, that of the bishop of Hereford who probably helped with the Inquest, states that the investigations had a dual character, for the king sent his officials to districts in which they themselves did not hold land to check the initial reports and advise the king if these had not been honestly compiled. It adds to the above that the number of ploughlands was also required, and that there was to be differentiation between 'those who dwelt in cottages and those who had their homes and a share in the fields', roughly the distinction between cottars and villeins in the Ely document above.

When the products of the Inquest first became known as 'Domesday Book' we do not know. In a few passages it styles itself *descriptio*, which can imply a 'writing down' as well as an account or description. It mentions also that the *descriptio* was made in the year 1086. But by 1179, and perhaps much earlier, the natives were calling it 'Domesday', the day of judgment. Elsewhere it is styled the 'Book of Winchester', for it was there that it was originally preserved. Now it rests in London in the Public Record Office. It does not cover the whole of the north of England, for much of the modern shires concerned were not then part of the English realm.

But it must be realised that it is not an altogether comprehensive document, for it omits much which we should be glad to have. Though space was left for them, the accounts of London, of Winchester, and of certain other towns, never became inscribed in the surviving text. In some shires, the ploughlands, the amount of arable land available, are not mentioned. The extent of pasture is rarely recorded for Norfolk and Suffolk. An appreciable number of estates are not named, and so often cannot be identified. In some entries a blank space was left for the number of the ploughlands, and sometimes we are not told the quantity of inhabitants of a manor. Fisheries are unmentioned in some counties in which they must surely have existed. It is unlikely that there was no woodland in north-western Berkshire, but none is recorded here, or that there were no slaves whatever on the Sussex estates of the archbishop of Canterbury. We can deduce, too, that the accounts of some manors were omitted. Also, the copying clerks not unnaturally made mistakes; e.g. they gave a sum in pounds when they should have written shillings, or placed an entry under the wrong heading. But it remains an unique record, and though it rarely states general principles, it is so detailed that it has enabled us to deduce much about life and conditions both before and after its compilation. With all its imperfections, it was a magnificent achievement, especially when we consider that it dealt with a country conquered by aliens only a score of years earlier and at a time when communications were poor.

It is written in Latin, but artificial Latin words had to be used for a number of technical terms, especially where there was no Norman-French equivalent for an English or Anglo-Danish word. The scribes of the day wrote by contracting words frequently employed, wherever possible, and also common terminations of Latin words and some of their syllables. But the handwritings of the record are largely clear and easy to read, and a small amount of practice soon enables one to interpret the text. It is, however, only fair to add that the somewhat telegraphic and formulistic language of Domesday Book sometimes makes correct interpretation hard to determine.

Three points need immediate emphasis. It was King William's contention that the whole of the country belonged to him, and that accordingly all men held their land of him. Thus one should not think of his barons and prelates as landowners, but rather as landholders or landlords.

Secondly, it is impossible to convert the values of Domesday Book into their equivalents in modern money. The value of money can be determined only in relation to current prices, and for only a few things, e.g. an ox, do we know what was regarded as their worth in the 11th century. What we might say is that the small man with an annual income of £10 was by no means badly off.

Thirdly, we speak of the 'Norman' Conquest. Normans held the bulk of English land after 1067, but there were also Bretons and Flemings, Frenchmen and Lotharingians, among the landholders of the time.

THE INQUEST

NO SINGLE PANEL of officials and clerks could have dealt with the whole country. The shires were grouped in at least seven, and perhaps nine, 'circuits'. Their composition has been deduced from the fact that formulae, order of arrangement of information, and presence or absence of certain detail, vary considerably, but are reasonably consistent for a particular area. The probable arrangement of the circuits was:

Kent, Surrey, Sussex, Hampshire, Berkshire

Wiltshire, Dorset, Somerset, Devon, Cornwall

Gloucestershire, Herefordshire, Worcestershire, Shropshire, Cheshire, south Lancashire

Oxfordshire, Warwickshire, Staffordshire, Leicestershire, Northamptonshire

Cambridgeshire, Bedfordshire, Hertfordshire, Middlesex, Buckinghamshire

Huntingdonshire, Derbyshire, Nottinghamshire, Yorkshire, Lincolnshire, Rutland

Essex, Suffolk, Norfolk

But despite this obvious local consistency no two shires within a circuit handled their information in exactly the same manner. Pasture was regularly noted in Essex, but rarely in Suffolk or Norfolk. Shropshire often uses a formula for stating the number of ploughlands which is absent from the Cheshire text. Cambridgeshire includes much information about Cambridge, but Bedfordshire devotes only a few lines to Bedford. Only one shire, Buckinghamshire, gives the lands of the late Queen Matilda a section separate from those of her husband. In Oxfordshire alone do we find a section concerned with the former estates of William fitzOsbern, who was killed in 1071.

The unit of organisation within the shire was that known as the

'Hundred', or in northern counties the 'wapentake'. Kent was further divided into 'lathes', Sussex into 'rapes', and Yorkshire and Lincolnshire into 'ridings', third parts or 'thridings'. Each contained a number of Hundreds or wapentakes, which differed enormously in size, while some consisted of the land belonging to the individual manor, especially where this was Church property. Except in the South-west, the name of the Hundred was inscribed before the manors within it, though numerous errors and omissions resulted. Adoption of the Hundred as the secondary territorial unit became reflected in the Domesday text. In some shires in which both bordars and cottars appear, only bordars are to be found under some Hundreds, only cottars in others. Documents based on the Inquest, but not reproduced in Domesday Book, treat them as a single class of the population. Two New Forest Hundreds have one formula for expressing the liability to tax of a manor, the others a different one.

Both shire and Hundreds held meetings, 'moots', of their chosen representatives, at regular intervals. These were required to assist at the Inquest. An Ely document shows that in Cambridgeshire and Hertfordshire eight men from each Hundred, four English and four 'French', formed the jury who gave evidence where the Inquest required it and swore to the truth of the statements submitted and set down in writing in the form of Domesday Book. This contains frequent reference to the testimony of shire- and Hundred-jury, to that of individuals, and occasionally to that of the 'men of the vill', the villeins. The Ely account of the terms of reference given above suggests that the priest, the reeve or overseer, and six villeins of each village had also to attest the truth of the information on oath. This they may well have done, but not, probably, in the presence of the inquisitors. It is more likely that when the basic information was being collected locally they did so on its completion. Not every hamlet could muster as many as six villeins, while many would have no priest or reeve. Moreover, for all such people to have attended the Inquest at the shire-town would have occupied more time than can be allowed for its probable duration. Their appearance would have had to be spread over many days.

The village, the 'vill' of Domesday, would indeed have proved to be an inconvenient unit for the Inquest. Some vills had land in more than one shire, e.g. Tidworth, which appears under Hampshire and Wiltshire; and we must suppose that there were two or more distinct settlements, though they went by a single name. A single name, moreover, might cover a wide extent of territory. In Devon 24 entries are all styled by slight variants of the name *Otri*, which represents the River Otter on which the settlements stood. Today these are represented by at least eight different places, and in 1086 these were in five different Hundreds. A village, too, might be shared between two or more lords, and while we may suppose that there were common fields for crop-growing, common pasture, and usually a single church, used by all, often there must in these instances have been more than one settlement, which would be slightly apart from each other. Some of these would not even have the status of a hamlet, but would be isolated farmsteads occupied only by the owner and his family. Others would represent former colonisations as the original village grew inconveniently large.

Sometimes separate settlements with a common name are distinguished in Domesday; we hear of Great Rollright and Little Rollright, of Snareshill and 'another Snareshill', of Cerne and Upcerne, further upstream than the parent settlement on the Cerne river. Later such places received distinguishing names; today we know Kings Nympton and Bishops Nympton, Brixton Deverill and Hill, Longbridge, Kingston, and Monkton Deverill, and where two or more parishes developed the dedication of the parish church sometimes differentiates them, as in Clyst St. Lawrence, Clyst St. George, and Clyst St. Mary.

So, despite frequent references to the vill, to 'pasture for the beasts of the vill', to 'the mill of the vill', this was not the Inquest's unit. Domesday itself makes this plain. If one man held two settlements with a common name, we should expect to find these portions of a village consecutive in the text. But often they are not; they must have been considered individually. If the vill had answered as a whole, we should expect the details to use the same units for each holding going by its name. But often we find the woodland or pasture of one given in acres, of another by linear measurements. Finally, many villages and hamlets which had a single owner were sometimes treated as an entity, and one set of totalled statistics given for the whole. For an entire Hundred might belong to the king or a bishopric or abbey.

The unit used for the Inquest was one which the authorities styled a manor, *manerium* or *mansio*. No simple definition of the term is possible, for manors differed enormously in character. In its elementary form a manor consisted of a single village or hamlet, or indeed of an isolated farm. But there were also many manors which were composed of a large number of properties, often at an appreciable distance from the one from which the manor took its name, treated for convenience by the owner as an economic and administrative unit. Some of these components are styled berewicks of the manor, places where produce was stored; of some it is said merely that they were 'members of' or 'lay in' a certain manor. In the northern shires estates from which the owner of a manor received the profits of justice, known as sokeland, were treated as part of the manor.

Sometimes the components of a complex manor are named. But more frequently we are afforded no clue to their whereabouts. This obviously militates against the satisfactory distribution of statistics among the parishes or villages concerned. The land of the manor of Finedon (220ai) lay in six named Northamptonshire Hundreds, but where, we are not told. That of some New Forest manors was at places unnamed but said to be in the Isle of Wight. Sometimes, however, we can deduce the components by reference to charters or other documents.

Often the clerk indicated that a holding was a manor, either by saying so or that it was held 'as a manor' or by inscribing a marginal M̄ for *manerium*. In some shires they used also their initials to indicate a berewick or sokeland. Moreover, when in the interests of efficiency the owner had combined several small properties into a single manor, the clerks said how many manors there had previously been, or wrote the appropriate figure over the symbol M̄. Often they noted that an estate had been added to a manor, or illegally abstracted from it by someone not its rightful owner. On occasion they stressed that an estate was not a manor or had not been held as a manor, or did not lie in any manor.

So the Inquest authorities must have considered it important to cause manorial status to be noted. Probably they did this because the manor had been and was the unit for liability to taxation and to duties such as the repair of roads and town walls. They did not wish anyone to be able to avoid his responsibilities, and it is not impossible that some alterations in the structure of manors had been made in the hope of escaping a portion of their liability. Possibly tax collectors had to visit each unit liable rather than receive the dues at the vill in which the Hundred-moot was held, and if so, a record of manors would be essential. This, too, may be why we find the terms 'hall' and 'court' as synonyms for 'manor', since payment would presumably be made at the owner's house. Yet occasionally we hear of manors which were 'without a hall', and this would be the situation when a manor had been leased as a whole to the peasantry, for their lord would be responsible for taxes collected from them.

The text is not, however, always entirely clear about manorial status. It reads sometimes as though a manor contained other manors, but it may well be that reference is really to holdings which had been manors before the Conquest but which had since been absorbed into a different manor.

Even houses within a town could be considered to be manors. But the accounts given of towns will here be dealt with separately. They differ enormously in content and volume, and are concerned with aspects of urban life quite different from those of the countryside.

We are not informed how most of the information incorporated in Domesday Book was provided. It cannot have been supplied by villagers visiting the shire-town to do so; this would have taken far too long. Since ultimately it was grouped according to landowners, it seems reasonable to suppose that it was collected by their stewards and reeves and bailiffs and that one or more of these attended the Inquest and supplied it to the clerks. These, too, would furnish details which were not the villagers' concern, such as manorial valuations. A few places seem to have failed to obey orders. No account was given of a portion of the bishop of Hereford's local estates; no reply was received from a Sussex holding (22a2), and none of the inhabitants of a Woodchester manor (164a2) attended the *descriptio*.

It is doubtful if the Inquest clerks visited each Hundred. It is more likely that the royal commissioners sat only in the shire-towns, or at most in a few convenient centres in the larger shires. Once it was thought that the original returns took the form of an account of each vill within a Hundred, that these were sent to Winchester, and then rearranged according to who held the land. From the first, it has been shown, the Inquest thought in terms of the individual's or institution's lands, whàt was styled a fief or 'honour'; the use of the Hundred was a matter merely of administrative convenience.

It is true that there has survived a 12th-century copy of an Inquest document which was drawn up in terms of the Hundred and the vill. This 'Inquest of the county of Cambridge' (*Inquisitio Comitatus Cantabrigiensis*), some of which is lost, includes much matter not to be found in Domesday Book, and deals with each Hundred as a whole and then with each vill within it. But it could not have been the source of Domesday Book for the county, for this includes information which is not present in the *Inquisitio*. This was probably a document made for a special purpose, and we have no suggestion that similar arrangements may have been produced for other counties.

A return by Hundreds and fiefs would presumably have recorded each property once only. But if each fief made its own return, each claimant, where a dispute existed, might include it in his return. Certainly Domesday Book contains a considerable number of parallel entries which deal with a single property, though these are rarely identical in wording or content, as is only to be expected if they had different sources. For example, Wilton nunnery reported that Richard Poingiant was tenant of some of the land of their manor of Chalke (68ai). But Richard must also have included it in his return under the name of Trow Farm in Alvediston parish (73a2), and gave a full acccount of it. He said he held it direct from the king, but Wilton claimed that he was only their tenant, not the landlord.

The Inquest appears to have been organised and held with extreme speed. It may have completed its work in less than eight months, some of which were winter months when travel would be at its most difficult. In the first instance notification of what was required had to be despatched to the sheriff of each shire, and he would then have to arrange for the local landowners and the Hundreds to be advised of the information they had to furnish. These had then to compile the requisite statistics, and we have to allow for the king's commissioners' time in travelling from one shire town to another. We know the names of the royal officials for one shire only, Worcestershire; they were the bishop of Lincoln and three leading barons who held no land locally. It is probable that they did not visit the provinces until the bulk of the problems had been argued before the shire- and Hundred-moots. It may be that the original intention was to leave the whole business to the authorities of each shire, but that the volume of claims and disputes proved so great, and the difficulties so insoluble, that it was decided to despatch unprejudiced officials of high rank to hear the conflicting evidence.

These must have had the status of royal justices, empowered to give verdicts where more than one person claimed an estate. If they did so, Domesday Book records their decisions only rarely. There are some notable exceptions, e.g. they relieved Tavistock Abbey of the manor of Werrington (101a2) because it had been a gift made after the Conquest by Gytha, widow of Earl Godwine, without the royal sanction. There is, for example, no indication in the text that Wilton had established its claim to Trow Farm. Indeed, sometimes the commissioners were unable to give a decision, and ruled that the case must go before the king himself, e.g. at Buckland (58bi) and about some Yorkshire estates (377bi).

Their judgments had to be based on the evidence of the shire- and Hundred-juries, often described as the 'men' or 'thegns' of the shire, or simply as 'the Hundred', and an immense number of entries record the statements these made. But upon occasion evidence was not forthcoming. Only one man 'out of the assembly of the whole shire' knew whether Westminster Abbey ought to possess Kelvedon (II.14b); the jurors 'knew nothing' about a holding near Witham (II.2), and in one case 'did not know how to tell the truth of it' (II.338).

The commissioners did not, however, rely entirely on these juries. They heard evidence from the sheriff, 'the men of the vill', 'the villeins of the manor', a reeve, the officials of an abbey, from a claimant's 'men'. Some of these were willing to support the truth of their statements by undergoing trial by battle or by subjecting themselves to the ordeal. They include a Hundred-jury, royal officials, an abbey's steward, 'men of the vill', and villeins, and not all of them were male. One Hampshire man was prepared to back his claim 'by the oath or ordeal of villeins and common folk and reeves', but his adversary relied on the oaths of 'the best and oldest men of the shire and Hundred', and presumably triumphed (44b2). To give evidence about a claim to part of Hayling Island by the bishop of Winchester, the aged abbot of Ramsey in Huntingdonshire, who had been a monk at Winchester, was summoned to appear.

Now there were various ways of establishing legitimacy of tenure. Some could produce the charters which bestowed the land upon them, some the 'writ and seal' of the king authorising the grant. Juries confirmed that they had seen the latter, or at least had heard it read out in the local court, for few of their members could read, though they might recognise the authenticity of a seal. When the lands of the English had been redistributed to those who profited by the Conquest is uncertain; the *Anglo-Saxon Chronicle* merely says that 'the king gave away every man's land' when he returned from Normandy at the end of 1067. The lands of ecclesiastical institutions were largely left undisturbed. Not only was King William a faithful supporter of the Catholic Church, but he needed the support and advice of his leading ecclesiastics. He indeed substituted foreign bishops and abbots for English ones whenever practicable, but on the whole the Church slightly increased its holdings in England.

His followers now had to be rewarded to a degree appropriate to their rank and value. But he did not immediately deprive all the English of their lands, only those who had fought against him or refused to submit to his authority. Enormous gifts of land and privileges were bestowed upon his half-brothers, Odo, bishop of Bayeux, and Robert of Mortain. His faithful intimate William fitzOsbern also received a vast number of English estates. The remainder were usually given the property of one or more Englishmen. Some of the most influential of these had held land in several shires (AElfstan of Boscumbe in Wiltshire had estates in eight), and in 1086 we find that most of the leading barons held estates in several counties. But for strategic reasons, and to control his lines of communication with Europe, he placed trusted friends in control of extensive districts. Odo of Bayeux was given much of Kent. Almost the whole of Sussex was shared between five major barons. Later he considered it judicious to guard his land frontiers by creating earldoms of Shrewsbury and Chester to combat the

Welsh menace, and by giving Alan of Brittany vast holdings in north Yorkshire. These Domesday Book styles his 'castlery', and we find in it mention of several other castleries (or 'divisions' or 'lowys') where a reliable magnate had been given a large block of local land for military purposes. King William of course succeeded to the Crown lands which had been held by Edward the Confessor, and he acquired the bulk of those owned by Earl Godwine and his family. Some of these, however, he bestowed on his principal adherents.

Many Englishmen had held only a few estates; thus the king's friends usually succeeded to the lands of several natives. The man who was succeeded was styled the newcomer's *antecessor*, and Domesday Book is full of statements indicating legality of tenure or otherwise by reference, often supported or denied by the testimony of shire and Hundred, to a baron's *antecessor*, the man whose lands he had been granted. Obviously the juries were in a position to state to whom a native's lands had been given, and could testify when possession was not in accordance with the royal wishes.

Another method of establishing legality of tenure at the Inquest was to invoke the evidence of the royal official who had formally put the new lord in possession of an estate, who had given him 'livery' or 'seizin' of it, as Domesday Book often says. The king's regents during his frequent absences in Normandy, Bishop Odo and William fitzOsbern, are frequently mentioned as conveying land, and so are the sheriffs and various trusted barons. Norman sheriffs replaced English officials as soon as was convenient, but before long the king was obliged to institute an enquiry into the misdemeanours the newcomers were committing.

But Domesday Book and other documents display what an appreciable amount of land was not being held as the king had ordained. Reference is made in them to numerous judicial proceedings instituted earlier in the reign to recover lands illegally appropriated. There had been major disputes between the archbishop of Canterbury and Odo of Bayeux and between the bishop of Worcester and the abbot of Evesham, and royal writs ordering restitution of property which had been usurped have survived. Among the worst sufferers was Ely Abbey, about whose lands litigation was frequent between 1071 and 1086, though some of her grievances had still not been settled when the Inquest was over. Many complaints arose from the fact that the Church had leased properties to laymen. The newcomers frequently appropriated such lands on the grounds that the holder had been their *antecessor*, and then claimed to hold it in chief; that is, with no superior lord but the king. However, the ecclesiastical institutions usually claimed that these holdings 'could not be separated from the Church'.

But whatever the wording of Domesday Book may suggest as regards legality of tenure, we frequently find the relevant entry placed among the land of the usurper, and not, except where there is a parallel entry, among that of the rightful owner. This suggests what is later to be considered here; the speed with which the Inquest was conducted implies that much of the record it produced was inscribed before the commissioners pronounced judgment, and it may be that often enough they did not do so. But often an estate is said to be 'in the king's hand', transferred to him to decide who should have it. A number of entries further suggest that sheriffs and the royal officials had been far from scrupulous in their allotment of estates. One of the principal sufferers from illegal acquisitions, it seems, had been the king himself.

Domesday Book is not always helpful about previous ownership. Manors are said to have been held by Earl Godwine or by Earl AElfgar of Mercia, who died before the Conquest, but who held them after their death is not stated. We cannot be sure that some estates had been Harold Godwineson's before the death of King Edward; some may indeed have been his own holdings, but others Crown lands. But the Domesday clerks, save for one slip when they wrote 'when Harold was reigning', treated him as an usurper, and William as Edward's legal and immediate successor. We are told very little about what must have been numerous changes in ownership between 1067 and 1086. Some of the newcomers had returned to Normandy, some had died, and some had lost their lands for complicity in the rebellion of 1075. One of the leading traitors had been Earl Roger of Hereford, William fitzOsbern's son, and because he lost his lands in consequence of his revolt we know little about what he may have held. We are, however, often informed about the estates of another leading rebel, Earl Ralf of East Anglia.

Nor does the text always reproduce the facts. It gives as landholders some men and women known to have been dead before the Inquest was over. Perhaps the account of their estates had already been inscribed, or these had not been transferred to their heirs before the entries were made. Certain charters show a transference of manors before 1086, the effects of which are ignored by the Domesday text. It makes practically no reference to the fall of Bishop Odo, imprisoned for disloyalty in 1082, and none to one of his leading adherents, Haimo de St. Clair, whom Ely documents show as holding much land in East Anglia. But it does most forcibly indicate how few natives still retained their possessions. Only two had substantial fiefs by 1086. But is is not unlikely that, though unmentioned, there were many who held their former manors as tenants of the new lords. We have to remember, too, that many Englishmen died at Stamford Bridge and Hastings, many revolted against King William after the Conquest, and many sought employment overseas.

Finally, the occasions on which information for all three dates specified in the Ely instructions is provided are comparatively rare except for Essex and East Anglia. For the most part we have the details for 1086 only.

A few facts derived from the record of one small county, Surrey, may give some idea of the inconsistencies of Domesday Book. In 21 entries no place-name is given, though that which might have been included can sometimes be identified. Many, though this is not said, may have been small components of manors; some give no information as to their equipment, and many only plough-teams, inhabitants, and values. All we are told about the vill of Putney (30bi) is the amount of toll it paid, and on the same folio the only information about Leatherhead is that it had a church. At least 16 passages additional to those dealing with the lands of sub-tenants indicate that a holding, sometimes named, was a component of a slightly distant manor. Many of these were portions of the enormous dispersed manor of Bramley, and others of Esher. Four entries mention land which was not in Surrey but in Kent, Sussex, or Hampshire (30a2 *bis*, 31ai, 34a2). Another three deal with land which did not belong to any manor. The hidage of one holding is not given; it is instead described as 'land for one plough-team' (31a2). Several entries note that what had been more than one manor was now a single manor, e.g. Burgh (32ai), Bletchingley (34bi), and Carshalton 36ai). Several holdings lay in a named Hundred but belonged to manors in other Hundreds.

Then there are stray pieces of information of a type rare in Domesday Book as a whole or in the circuit in which Surrey had been. There are five instances of the practice of commendation, of attaching oneself to a superior for protection and becoming his 'man' (32ai, 32bi,2, 36ai,bi). Sokeright, the privilege of receiving the fines for offences committed by a subordinate, appears thrice (32ai, 35b2, 36ai). Other unusual items are the existence of croft (Ewell, 30 bi), a *cultura terrae* (? a small piece of cultivated land — Lambeth, 34a2), trial by battle (Pickets Hole, 36b2), a royal smith (Carshalton, 36a2), land received as a marriage portion (Carshalton, 36a2), and the dating of a tenure as 'when the king was in Wales', which he was in 1081.

As an indication of deficiencies, it may be added that in 35 entries a blank was left where the quantity of the ploughlands should have come, and while, if a holding was a component of a manor, this was normally given as covering the whole arable land of the manor, there are at least 40 passages from which the information is absent.

4

THE KING'S GELD

TAXATION, and liability for certain common burdens such as the upkeep of fortresses and bridges, and military service, had for long been based not on the actual capabilities of manor or vill, but on an unit known as the 'hide'. The hide was something originally conceived of as the average agricultural holding of a peasant household or family-unit. It was divided into four quarters or 'virgates', and arithmetically, though probably not often physically, into 120 acres, though in 1086 we find hides as accounting units of 40 or 48 acres in the South-west. All these fit in well with a money system which reckoned 240 pence to the pound. The virgate could also be divided into ferdings or ferlings, 'fourth parts' thereof, and there was a Cornish geld-acre which seems to have been reckoned as one-third of the virgate, but of 64 of the areal acres of other districts. In the shires settled by Danish invaders we have carucates, not hides, also of 120 acres, the fourth part of which was the 'yoke' and the eighth the 'bovate'. The carucate must have been derived from the land for one plough-team or *caruca* of eight oxen, which was reckoned to be capable of ploughing an acre in a forenoon, and the bovate from that for one ox. In Kent the unit was the sulung, divided into yokes, and this seems to have been roughly the equivalent of two hides.

The use of the hide as an unit goes far back into English history. A very early document known as the *Tribal Hidage* allots large quantities of hides to the various territories of early peoples. Another, the *County Hidage*, does the same for 13 shires, but the figures are rarely close to those of Domesday Book. Sometimes, however, they are of as many hundred hides as there were Hundreds in a shire, though nowhere did a Hundred necessarily consist of 100 hides. There were double Hundreds of 200 hides, 'Hundreds and a half' of 150, and many with less than 100 hides.

At some time the hidage of a shire had been fixed, and that of its Hundreds also, but many figures were probably varied later. Hundreds had apportioned their quotas between the vills within them, presumably in accordance with their capacities, and on a decimal basis. Vills would be given five, ten, or some other decimal quantity of hides, or combined to give similar ratings for two or more of them. In shires in which the carucate was the unit, the basis was duodecimal, and an assessment of six carucates on the vill was the norm.

At the time of the Inquest we still find many vills rated at these figures or their multiples. But where there were a number of holdings making up the vill, we find every kind of fraction of integers as the assessments of the various holdings. These were perhaps once realistic. No doubt all assessments had once been based roughly on the size and character of the vill. But by 1086 we find vills with equal numbers of hides but differing widely in population, agricultural capacity, and value, for the life of the countryside had not been static. There must have been much colonisation, some clearing of the waste land, woodland and scrub, while agricultural or military disaster would have affected some vills since the time when the original ratings were fixed.

In East Anglia, though here we find carucates also, these were not units of assessment, but rather represent the ploughlands, which are never named. Villages had been grouped in what were called 'leets', and liability to taxation is indicated by a statement that to every 20 shillings of tax for which the Hundred was liable, the holding had to contribute so many pence.

The land-tax of Anglo-Danish England was known as 'geld'. There could be various forms of geld; to buy off invading Danish armies, to maintain professional soldiers and sailors, and to form a portion of the royal revenue. The last was probably a normal annual tax, and was frequently levied at the rate of two shillings on the hide. But that for which accounts remain had been at thrice that sum.

Now the liability of every holding must have been available in writing and known to all sheriffs and their officials, who were responsible for the collection of geld and its transport to the royal treasury. But one of the Inquest's tasks was to ensure that full liability was recorded. Thus the first item of concrete information after the name of the holding and holder in Domesday Book is the number of hides or carucates for which it gelded or 'defended itself' — defended itself against dangers from abroad and the imposition of penalties for non-payment or evasion. It was the lord's responsibility to collect their shares from his tenants and villagers and pay it over to the collectors.

The country contained something like 70,000 hides and carucates. But not all these were liable for geld. Many royal manors did not pay, for instead they had to make large contributions, originally of provisions, to support a king and his household who were constantly travelling throughout the land as these visited their district. Some of these are said never to have assessed or never to have gelded. A large number of manors had at varying times obtained partial exemption. Many of these belonged to the Church, and piety must have been responsible for some of its immunities. Some might have been made partially exempt in order to gain or ensure the support of an influential landowner. But there were other reasons for exemption also. Fareham (40bi) had its assessment reduced by one-third 'because it was on the sea' and suffered from piratical raids. That of Chippenham (197a2) was halved because it could not manage to pay the full geld and also make its contribution, as a royal manor, to the king's revenue.

The amount of exemption is given in Domesday Book in varying ways. In the south-eastern shires, where a holding had total or partial exemption, we are told that it gelded for so many hides 'then', but for a lower quantity 'now'. The first must indicate the original or an earlier assessment, the second that for which geld was actually paid. But there are also instances where phrases such as 'now they have not gelded' may imply failure to pay at the last levy.

Exempted land was often described as being 'in demesne', *in dominio*, and this is the formula used in the geld accounts of the South-west. Though often the amount coincides with land said in Domesday Book to be in demesne, it frequently does not. The probability is that the amount of land in demesne of a manor was inclined to fluctuate, and certainly tenancies had been created out of it, but the amount exempt, fiscal as opposed to manorial demesne, remained fixed and traditional. The demesne is properly the lord's home farm as distinct from the land of the villeins and

any sub-tenancies. In the Cornish Exeter text we are usually given
the amount of manorial demesne, but also the hidage of the whole
manor and a statement that the manor gelded for a smaller
quantity, the difference between these being fiscal demesne.
Though in circuits other than the above we are sometimes told
how much does not geld, for the most part we are given manorial
demesne only, and not always this.

Some immunities were probably of considerable antiquity. The
100 hides of Chilcombe (41ai) had defended themselves for a
single hide since the days of AEthelred (d. 1016), perhaps since
those of AEthelwulf (d. 858), and Wenlock (252bi) secured partial
exemption during Cnut's reign. The granting of immunities by
both King Edward and King William are mentioned in Domesday
Book, and the shire and Hundred upon occasion testified to the
legality of claims for exemption.

The figures of the County Hidage suggest that many shires had
enjoyed substantial general reductions between its date and that of
Domesday Book. Northamptonshire seems to have been relieved
of about half its obligation, and the reason may have been the
savage treatment it had received during the Northumbrian revolt
against Earl Tostig Godwineson in 1065. Some Cambridgeshire
Hundreds had had the assessment of each vill cut by 20%.
Inequality of treatment is obvious. The Isle of Wight and
Middlesex had much the same number of hides, while Wiltshire,
with over 4,000, compares unfavourably with its neighbours
Dorset and Somerset, which have far less.

Domesday Book uses another term also to denote exempted
land, 'inland' as opposed to 'warland', the latter being that which
gelded, 'defended itself' by contribution to a tax often devoted to
the defence of the realm. It makes it clear, too, that land within a
royal Forest did not pay geld, for either the former inhabitants
had been transferred elsewhere or the restrictions the Forest laws
placed on their agricultural activities made them incapable of
paying.

We find carucates in districts other than those settled by the
Danes. Domesday Book covers certain areas which had not been
part of the English realm, and so had never been assessed in hides.
These include the Welsh borderland in which the Normans were
organising castleries for frontier defence and offence. Especially in

the South-west 'carucates of land which were not divided into hides and never gelded' appear. They are paralleled by instances elsewhere of demesne land for varying quantities of plough-teams additional to the hides noted. They may represent grants of land or reclamation from the waste subsequent to the latest assessment, and which needed to be reported for fear of loss if they were not claimed at the Inquest.

In the northern shires which had been settled by the Danes we find a special use of the terms 'hide' and 'Hundred'. 12 carucates made a 'Hundred', but there are Leicestershire instances of six, seven, and eight units of six carucates. Here, too, we find 'hides' which were composed of 18 carucates, and in south Lancashire 'hides' of six carucates. All originate in the duodecimal system of reckoning. Two passages in the account of Lincoln refer to computation 'in the English way, that is, 100 for 120', so that 1,150 houses were reckoned as 970, and 240 as 200.

A normal geld seems often to have been at the rate of two shillings upon each hide; the six-shilling geld of 1085/6 was an abnormally high one. But a Berkshire passage (56bi) speaks of a geld of seven pence paid in two equal instalments before Christmas and at Pentecost.

5

THE PLOUGHLAND AND THE PLOUGH-TEAM

THE AMOUNT of land for which there were plough-teams in a manor was of obvious importance, though it was not one of the items in the Ely document which seems to list the information required by the Inquest. Indeed, no mention of ploughlands, or only occasional quantities, occur in some shires. The normal formula is that 'there is land for' so many teams, but often, especially in the South-east, a blank space was left where the quantity should have come. An alternative formula gives the number of plough-teams, and adds that there could be employed so many teams more. The implication is that the total of these gives the number of ploughlands. For the formula is used also in some shires where this is stated, and in most instances the teams plus the number of potential teams equals the ploughlands. In Leicestershire four formulae appear, the two above, and two giving the number of teams there had been at an earlier date. Some fiefs used one, and some another.

In some shires the quantities of ploughlands given are obviously artificial ones. In Rutland symmetrical figures are apparent. In Alstoe wapentake there are 24 carucates and land for 48 plough-teams, but 84 ploughlands are recorded, on which there were 101½ plough-teams. The manor of Oakham (293b2) had 39 plough-teams for its 16 ploughlands, and yet four more teams could have been employed. There seems to be no doubt that in several shires the ploughlands do not represent arable land at all, but an earlier basis for taxation based on a duodecimal system. This is particularly marked in Northamptonshire, where in one part of the county the hides are 40% of the number of ploughlands, in another 50%.

In the carucated shires there is often a mathematical relationship between carucates and ploughlands, which probably originated in changes in the system and intensity of assessments. In some holdings the ploughlands and carucates are equal in number, in others the number of ploughlands is half that of the carucates, in others two-thirds.

Thus the agricultural capacity of England in 1086 cannot be determined. Yet the clerks seem to have felt that there should be a plough-team for each ploughland. Frequently they wrote 'there is land for one team, and the team is there'. In contrast, when, as they often had to record, there were more teams than ploughlands, they made such entries as 'there is land for two teams, and yet there are three teams there'. For a number of large manors they seem to have arrived at the quantity of ploughlands by adding together the demesne teams, those of the sub-tenants, and those of the villagers. Presumably the number of the ploughlands had not been provided, for it seems improbable that immense and dispersed manors such as Crediton (101b2) had 185 ploughlands and 185 plough-teams. So many large manors are credited with round numbers of 50 or 100 ploughlands that the figures cannot represent reality. On some of these there are less than half as many plough-teams as there are ploughlands. Yet at Otterton (104b2) there were 46 teams but only 25 ploughlands, and we cannot think that 21 teams were maintained in idleness.

Of some of these discrepancies there are possible explanations. In some manors only one-half or one-third of the land may have been ploughed in any one year, the remainder being left fallow to recover from crop-growing. Sometimes we seem to be given the ploughlands of the demesne and of the villeins, but not those of the sub-tenancies, though the teams of the latter are recorded. Many a small estate has its ploughlands noted, but no teams are mentioned. There must have been a good deal of hiring of teams, and of co-operation to form the full team of eight oxen, for many an unimportant landholder is said to have possessed only one or two oxen. A surplus of teams may have been a profitable acquisition, for men with insufficient oxen must hire to get their land tilled. Uffington (366b2) was ploughed by the teams of Belmesthorpe (346a2), and the villeins and their oxen of Newsellsbury ploughed at Barley (139ai). Collation of the Exeter text with the Exchequer version shows that the clerks of the latter were not scrupulous about quantities: three or five oxen in the former appear as half a team in the latter.

On the whole, there seem to have been fewer plough-teams available than could have been used. The ravages of war (and there were several revolts and invasions after the Conquest), animal disease, and poverty would all reduce the number of oxen in use. An army on the march could feed itself only by requisitioning and slaughtering what beasts it could find and acquire. In some places a lord may have found sheep- or pig-farming more profitable than crop-growing on all the arable land at his disposal.

6

THE SLAVES AND THE PEASANTRY

DESPITE ITS WEALTH of statistics, Domesday Book does not enable us to arrive at a really close estimate of the total population of 11th-century England. We are without figures for some holdings, we can form no conception of how many inhabitants there may have been in the cities undescribed, or in the parts of the country the Inquest did not cover. We know little of the possible numbers of cathedral clergy, monks and nuns, garrisons, or government officials. We do not know the average size of the family, or whether grown-up sons were counted and the elderly and infirm excluded. Thus a potential population of 1¼ million might be somewhat wide of the mark.

Nor can we always allot the persons mentioned to a particular class. Occasionally a quantity indivisible between the categories mentioned is given, e.g. that there are eight 'between the free men and the villeins' (Sutton, 252b2). The number of female slaves recorded is so small, only a little over 600, that we can but think that there must have been many more than the figures would suggest. In 20 counties none is mentioned. A smith may not necessarily have been a villein, and in any case only 71 are recorded, so the remainder must be concealed under the heading of other classes. While we read of a number of occupations, e.g. in fishing or apiculture, not mentioned in the Ely document, we do not know what status to allot to those who practised them. Often enough a priest seems to have been of the villein class, but there were also priests who were quite substantial landholders. Since only about 900 in all are mentioned, and some shires list only one or two, there must have been many who were not specified as having been priests. Over 600 persons are styled merely 'men', *homines*; reeves mentioned as such number only 56, shepherds 10, and there are only two carpenters and half a dozen millers. It is a vivid indication of how few manors reported their inhabitants by trade or occupation. But we must remember that few men would be concerned with their speciality during all their working hours. They had labour in the fields and many other tasks to perform.

Domesday Book does not tell us how the various categories of the population occupied their time, though occasionally it gives glimpses of their responsibilities and privileges. There must have been large differences in the status and prosperity of the men styled 'villeins', and probably of those of other classes also. For indication of their equipment and duties we are dependent on manorial surveys and certain other documents compiled both before and after the Conquest. On neither social nor economic grounds can we clearly separate the broad divisions of Domesday Book.

In most entries slaves, *servi*, come last in the order of inhabitants, or are associated with the demesne plough-teams, for so far as we can tell they had no oxen of their own and did the majority of the work on the demesne. Though the slave was regarded as a thing rather than as a person, he does not seem to have been altogether without rights. He had some free time, and could work for pay in it; he might indeed save enough to purchase his freedom. He may even have had an acre of land of his own, and he received an annual allowance of food. Ploughing would have been his principal occupation, but some entries record a solitary slave as the sole inhabitant of an isolated outpost. On such minute holdings he may have been engaged in herding sheep or swine.

More than 28,000 male slaves are mentioned in Domesday Book. That these were all who were in existence is improbable. Many a large manor on which we should expect to find slaves, and which possessed demesne teams, was apparently without them. They do not appear on any of the archbishop of Canterbury's extensive manors in Sussex, though there were plenty of slaves elsewhere on his property. None is mentioned in the Yorkshire and Lincolnshire texts, and very few in neighbouring counties. It may be that in the shires influenced by Danish settlement, with their high proportion of free peasants, slavery had virtually died out, or that districts deliberately devastated after their revolts against Norman government were too poor to support slaves. But though none is noted in Huntingdonshire, the Ely Inquest, undoubtedly based on Inquest material, lists them for all the manors of Ely Abbey, and thus the record of the northern circuit may be deceptive. It is hard to think that the extractive industries of the North, e.g. lead-mining, operated without some slave-labour.

Another difficulty in estimating the number of slaves is that we do not know whether they were reckoned as individuals, or whether, as apparently was the system for other classes of the population, only the senior male of a family was counted. Some have thought that only those slaves concerned with definite domestic offices were returned. Two men were needed to operate the plough-team, and commonly we find the slaves on a manor double the number of teams. This may suggest that they were not counted as individuals.

Though traffic in slaves was still active (we are told that at Lewes the toll on the sale of a man was fourpence), their numbers seem to have been falling. In the eastern counties, where frequently we are given figures for 1066 and for 1086, and sometimes for an intermediate date, this is markedly apparent. In Essex their numbers had declined by about 30%. Now the emancipation of slaves had long been encouraged as a Christian action, and we hear that at Hailes (167bi) 12 had been freed. Economic motives must also have affected their numbers. The aged slave, or the sick slave, was a complete liability. It was sound policy to give some slaves their freedom and encourage them to become self-supporting by giving them a limited means of subsistence.

The text mentions *coliberti* in a few entries. The term seems to denote a number of slaves freed simultaneously. They are found only in the South and West, and no more than about 850 appear, or 3% of the relevant total for slaves. Some could apparently pay quite considerable rents and own an appreciable number of plough-oxen, as at Kingsclere (39a2) and Cosham (38a2). There may well have been many more than were recorded, for if they now had a little land and occasional oxen, the clerks may have classed them among the far more numerous bordars. The Eardisland coliberts (179b2) were required to give the lord quantities of corn and barley, sheep and lambs, and a small rent. There are also a few persons styled *buri* or 'boors', and in three entries this seems to be an alternative term for colibert.

The extent of slavery varied enormously both in geographical distribution and according to the landowner. The percentage of slaves increases markedly as we go from East to West, though an abnormally low figure in Sussex may be the result of their deliberate omission from some fiefs. It is rarely high on the royal estates; often, but by no means invariably, low on those of the Church, who might have been expected to give a lead in their emancipation. But here and there we find an ecclesiastical institution with a high proportion of slaves. It approached 30% on the Somerset manors of Bath Abbey, but on the Glastonbury estates in that shire was about 11%. But percentages might often depend on the proportions of demesne land and the extent to which land was let to lay tenants.

In the Welsh border shires there were considerable numbers of *bovarii*, who must have been 'oxmen' and principally concerned with ploughing. They may have been servile, though sometimes slaves and oxmen are found together on the same manor, for a few times we hear of a 'free oxman'. These oxmen represent nearly one-quarter of the total of slaves plus oxmen in the limited area in which they appear. The number of slaves in the districts nearest Wales is not large, so Welsh captives in war do not seem to have been forced into slavery in large number. On the other hand, slaves of Welsh origin may have been ignored.

The exact status of coscets, cottars, and bordars, the first two of which do not occur in all counties, is indefinable. They came below the villeins in status, and the coscet seems to have been inferior to the cottar. Between the cottar and bordar some clerks saw no distinction; when they summarised totals they added the figures for these together and styled the sum 'bordars'. Some districts record only cottars, others only bordars. It is suggestive that while well over 80,000 bordars can be counted, cottars are not greatly in excess of 5,200, and coscets fewer than 1,750, while the use of the latter term in the South-west, in which almost all the coscets appear, seems to have been limited to certain areas.

What made those responsible classify the peasantry in this manner is also indeterminable. Cottars and bordars suggest those who dwell, not in the village, but in cottages some little distance away. But it would probably be wrong to say that this always differentiated them from villeins.

The extent of the holdings of cottars is sometimes given. It rarely exceeded five acres and was often considerably less. Some are said to have had no land except for their 'gardens', but there are indications that a rent of about one shilling for these could be found by the individual. The majority can have owned no plough-oxen, but we do find some who possessed an ox, and so did certain coscets.

The normal holding of a bordar seems to have been five acres, though many had less, and we find some in Middlesex who had 15. There are many entries which show that there were plenty of bordars who owned no oxen, and if we could arrive at a comprehensive average we should probably find that this did not exceed one ox per man. We find also holdings on which they averaged four, but these must have been exceptional. Some could furnish modest rents, e.g. at Larkton (264bi), which was one of two shillings, but others are stigmatised as 'poor' or 'having nothing'.

Some may have been enfranchised slaves. This might at times be so where we find bordars on a holding, but no slaves. Though the figures in the eastern counties amply indicate that the huge increase in their numbers could not be entirely due to that cause, for in Essex alone they rose from 3,864 to 6,303, it probably compensates to some extent for the decline of slavery in this district. The amount of work they were by custom obliged to do on their lord's land must have been considerably greater than that of the villeins. But they had leisure in which to cultivate their own land, and to labour for pay on that of men of status and wealth greater than theirs. But every man prepared to sell his labour during his free time was subject to the extent of local demand. There cannot have been permanent opportunity to earn money.

Well over 100,000 villeins appear. The term is of course a highly elastic one, for not only were there well-to-do villeins besides those certainly no better off than the best equipped bordars, but the villein must often have been a tradesman and a technician with special responsibilities in the manorial economy. The villein, *villanus*, is in the essence the villager, the most important element in village life. Again it is obvious that not all areas treated him in the same fashion. In Gloucestershire there are over twice as many villeins as there are bordars and cottars and coscets, and they made up nearly half the peasant population; in its neighbour Wiltshire villeins total less than do the above three categories.

The duties of villeins are but rarely mentioned, and would vary from manor to manor. We read of them having to plough some of the lord's land and sow it with seed they themselves provided (Leominster, 180ai) and mow the meadow (Grafton, 175ai), yet at Kingstone (179bi) 'the villeins . . . carried venison to Hereford and did no other service'. Pre- and post-Conquest surveys tell us something more of what must normally have been multifarious obligations to their lords. They had to perform guard and escort duties, cart loads, wash and shear sheep, thrash the corn, and cut and cart timber, help with the ploughing of the demesne, its cultivation, and its harvest. Indeed, a statement for Luffenham (219a2) might apply to many a manor: 'the men labour . . . as the reeve shall command'.

The normal holding of a villein in the common fields seem to have been regarded as the virgate of 30 acres, but 15-acre plots were not uncommon. In any village there must have been wide disparity in their equipment. There must, if we are reading the text aright, have been many villeins who owned no plough-oxen, yet some seem to have possessed four or even more. But we cannot strike a true average, for too often plough-teams are given as so many 'between the lord and his men', or 'between the villeins and bordars' and several other named categories, often superior to the villeins. One calculation would allot three oxen to the average villein.

It is probable that some of the villeins of 1086 were former free men who had sunk in the social scale as a result of the Conquest. This was certainly so at Benfleet (II.1b), where a free man was 'made one of the villeins'. There is mention of 'free villeins' (Barford, II.145) who may have been former free men. There are numerous notices of villeins' land having been converted to a sub-tenancy and bestowed upon a powerful baron's adherent. But this may not imply that the villagers had suffered a loss. There may since the Conquest have been too few villeins to maintain it.

Yet some villeins could afford to rent whole manors, e.g. at Alverstoke (41bi), and pay substantial rents for them. The ten at Lympstone (113ai) paid £8, assisted perhaps by the six bordars mentioned, and here there were two slaves. They could rent fisheries at Ruyton (257b2), and they possessed fisheries on the Severn (164ai) and woodland at Rothley (230ai). The rents they paid for land are occasionally specified, though it is not always stated that the sums mentioned represent the rents paid. A rent of one penny per acre seems to have been common (e.g. at Fanton, II.17b). We hear of dues in money and in kind payable for the pasturing of sheep and swine: in Sussex (16bi) one pig in every seven became the lord's in return for the exercise of this amenity; elsewhere the proportion might vary. Pasture-rents were sometimes discharged in the form of hens (Guiting, 167b2), sheep (Hatfield Broad Oak, II.2), ploughshares (Abington, 199b2), or iron (Whitestaunton, 91b2). Such dues naturally varied with the character of the manor. The men of Wilburton (192ai) paid 16 pence to be allowed to gather rushes with which to make rush-lights and cover floors, eel-rents were common, and so were dues settled by the provision of salmon and sea-fish, grain, and honey for sweetening. At Marcle (179b2) the villeins had to find 17 shillings for fish, eight shillings for salt, and 65 shillings for honey. These may represent the commutation of provender-dues in cash. In Archenfield (179b2), a district south of Herefordshire and largely Welsh, an ox had to be surrendered as death duty when a villein died.

Occasionally we hear of 'half-villeins'. The term must denote a man who had obligation to work on more than one holding, and not a man who was semi-free.

7

THE FREE PEASANTRY AND THE LOWER MIDDLE CLASSES

DOMESDAY BOOK mentions numerous categories of men, often in only one or two entries for a county, who may be classed as somewhat superior to villeins, though the obligations of many of these do not seem to have differed substantially from those of villeins. The difference was probably one of status rather than of economic freedom. Their position in the entries brigades them with the peasantry rather than with the native survivors who still held small estates direct from the king. Thus we hear of men who in 1086 still went by the title of 'thegn', and the 'drengs' found only in south Lancashire seem to be their equivalent. They had services to perform just as the villeins and bordars had, though far less arduous or continuous. For example, they had to 'make the king's house as the villeins do' (possibly a temporary hunting-lodge), construct fences to restrict the movement of deer, and help with reaping the royal crops (269b2). Of the duties of most other classes mentioned, e.g. *servientes* or sergeants, franklins, and unnamed Englishmen, we can learn practically nothing.

The only category who are noted in substantial quantity are those styled radmen or radknights. Between 500 and 600 are recorded, almost all in the shires bordering or near Wales. They were 'riding men', whose duties included journeying on their lord's errands and escort work, but they also had to convey goods and produce and perform a limited amount of agricultural service, e.g. ploughing, harrowing, mowing. Their distribution in the relevant shires suggests further that they may have had obligations connected with the chase. It is on occasion specifically stated that they were free men. They held on the whole more land and possessed more plough-oxen than the average villein, often from a half to a whole hide and from four to eight oxen, though there are radmen who seem to have been without oxen.

Welshmen are not often mentioned, but in any case only those living on land which was part of the English realm would be recorded. Most of them seem to have been renting land for small sums and rendering dues of honey, sheep, or the hawks required for the chase. Those of whom we are told had anything up to a full team of eight oxen. The Normans were pressing beyond the previous borders to strengthen their frontiers and exploit new land, and we hear of payments from Welsh districts beyond the limits of the shires from Gloucestershire to Cheshire. Robert of Rhuddlan, cousin to Earl Hugh of Chester, had with his relative extended Norman authority deep into North Wales. Chepstow, Caerleon, and Monmouth castles and castleries each receives brief mention.

Some of the numerous categories mentioned in Domesday Book are best considered when manorial equipment is studied (Chapters IX and X), e.g. swineherds and fishermen. Some terms are too vague to allow of definition, e.g. 'rustics' (*rustici*); some are recorded by their special occupation, e.g. potters, iron-workers, and dairymaids.

Then there are the *milites*, who varied greatly in status and possessions. The term is usually translated as 'knight', but many a *miles* was very far from our conception of the medieval knight. In many entries a better translation would be 'trained soldier', a baron's trusted fighting man of the non-commissioned officer type who had been given a small estate by his lord. But some had quite substantial holdings, sometimes as much as five hides, and possessed several plough-teams. These are not so very different from the named sub-tenants who frequently held considerable portions of manors and had members of the peasantry to work for them. Not all were newcomers, for some are said to be English, and before the Conquest thegns at Feckenham (180bi) had had *milites* under them who were as free as themselves.

We are not given the names of many of the landholders of 1066, nor is differentiation frequently made between men of the same name. But their nicknames and distinguishing epithets — sometimes untranslatable — are occasionally given, as 'the Dane, 'the swarthy', 'the bald', and so is their parentage. Too frequently we are told simply that one or more thegns or free men had holdings in the enlarged pre-Conquest manor which often each of

these had held as a manor in 1066. The holdings of sokemen are
also recorded, and again we are often merely told their number
and how much they held between them.

In most entries we are informed in what manner they had held
their land. The terms used vary; they had held it 'as a manor' (*pro
manerio*), 'freely' (*libere*), 'in parage' (*in paragio*), or as an 'alod'.
Collation of the material suggests that tenure in parage was the
equivalent of holding land as a manor; holding freely may well
imply the same. Nothing suggests that holding by allodial tenure
(reported only in the South-east, though the other terms are used
here also), differed substantially from holding freely. Sometimes
we are told that estates were not so held, and these we must think
had been but components of a manor.

We are moreover frequently told that the holder of an estate
could or could not give or sell his land, 'go with his land' to a
different lord from the one with whom he was associated, or
'recede' from him. It had been a principle of English land-law that
there should be no land without its lord, and that every man
should have his lord. The lord might be male or female. The great
man would have no lord but the king, the lesser man 'commended'
himself to one more powerful than himself. The legal implications
of the tie of commendation are not clear, but we may suppose
that the one received protection and support, and perhaps working
capital on loan, livestock and implements, the other an adherent in
war and peace. The tie was not indissoluble, for many commended
men, the text tells us, could change their lord at will. When Edric
of Laxfield, among the greatest men in the eastern counties in the
Confessor's day, was outlawed and exiled, Godric the priest, who
had been commended to him, became the man of Northmann. A
man seems to have been able to commend himself to several
different lords simultaneously. We find instances of the possession
of every fraction of a man's commendation from one-sixth
upwards.

But there were also many holdings the tenant of which could
not sell or transfer his land. Sometimes he could do so if he
obtained his lord's leave for the transaction, but usually it was
either categorically stated that he could not sell it, or leave his
lord, or that it always 'lay in' a bishopric or abbey or manor. For
ecclesiastical institutions especially could not afford to allow their

tenants to quit their responsibilities, nor would laymen be anxious for them to do so. The holders of such lands had definite services to perform, and one of these may well have been serving in the body of armed men which the lord of the fief had to provide when the king summoned it. There are several references to compulsory military service in Domesday Book. In Berkshire one fighting man had to be furnished for every five-hide unit, and that this was the norm is suggested by the statement that one man had to be found by Malmesbury (64bi) in respect of five hides. Each fief no doubt had its local quota, based on a rough equation of one man from each five hides. The bishop of Worcester had to find 60 soldiers in respect of his 300 hides in the shire.

Such land was often styled 'thegnland', though it need not necessarily be tenanted by a thegn. For originally the ownership of five hides had qualified a man to be considered as of thegnly status. The terms of tenancy were usually those of a lease, though sale of the land is also mentioned, but normally there were qualifications. The lease was frequently for the term of three lives, of the lessee, his son, and his grandson. It has been mentioned earlier that the newcomers had been appropriating thegnland on the grounds that their *antecessor* had held it, and in consequence Domesday Book is full of the registration of claims that this land could not pass out of the landholder's control. It is because of this that so much was recorded stating whether a man could sell his land and leave his lord, for one outstanding feature of King William's land-settlement was that the newcomer must accept not only the privileges of his *antecessor*, but his responsibilities also. Yet we read of surprising latitude in the system. A man bought land at Highway (72a2) from Malmesbury Abbey 'for three lives', but during the period of his lease he could 'go with the land to what lord he pleased'. Purchase is obviously conditional, not outright purchase. But King William's settlement included a further important feature. Before the Conquest, men had held their land 'under' some superior. Now they held it 'of' the king or a tenant-in-chief, with restriction on a transfer of loyalties.

Over 14,000 free men, and more than 23,000 sokemen, were still holding land in 1086. More than 80% of those recorded are to be found in the three eastern counties. To draw a precise dividing line between them is impossible. It is most unlikely that there

were no free men in Lincolnshire, where there were 11,000
sokemen, yet that is what the text says. In some entries the two
appear to be indistinguishable, for once we read of 'a free man
who was wholly a sokeman' (II.353), and sometimes persons who
are sokemen in Domesday Book are free men in the Ely Inquest
based on similar material. Equally the person styled 'free man'
might also be a thegn, as in the two Melton villages (II.204b). We
cannot say that the free man is 'more free' of obligations than the
sokeman, or that he is the more prosperous of the two. For they
varied in the extent of their land just as villeins did. We find a free
man with as much as four carucates at Great Bircham (II.222b),
but one with only a quarter-acre at Hoo (II.317b). A Denton
sokeman had two carucates and ten acres (II.390), and this was
classed as a manor, one at Dursley could sell his land (132b2), and
one at Writtle (II.5) could 'go with his land where he would', yet
18 at Islington (II.213) had only 17½ acres between them.

The inequalities in the importance of free men and sokemen is
manifested also in the numbers of plough-oxen ascribed to them.
While some of the former had anything from a half to an entire
team, not all possessed a single beast, and the groups we often
encounter, who must have varied in possessions with the
individual, frequently had but few oxen. At West Dersham
(II.274) 32 had only two teams between them. The sokemen show
similar figures. Some, but not very many, owned a whole team,
but there were plenty without oxen, and a group-average of less
than an ox per man is common.

The free man might have other free men under him, as at
Mettingham (II.300b), though he was indeed commended to
someone superior to himself. Apparently the sokeman might have
sokemen under him (Hemblington, II.129). Men are found
commended to someone who is himself commended to a superior.
It may be that the free man was more independent of the control
of a lord or manorial organisation than the sokeman, and that he
was slightly superior socially. Though many a sokeman seems to
have been less prosperous than the best-equipped villein, he
certainly stood higher in the social scale.

Something over 100 *francigenae* are mentioned. The proper
translation is not necessarily 'French-born', for these may be the
equivalent of *liberi homines*, free men. Once we hear of a *francus*

teinus, and a 'French thegn' would be a contradiction in terms.

Whatever independence freeman and sokeman may have possessed before the Conquest seems to have been largely lost afterwards. Their holdings may earlier have been free of obligations to estates larger than their small farms, but by 1086 many of them had been absorbed into the newcomers' manors, and presumably had to furnish limited labour service. The enormous 'sokes' which we find in the North and East associated with individual manors could readily become mere adjuncts of the manor, not independent farms.

Certainly the number of free men and sokemen appears to have decreased since the Conquest, and not entirely because of mortality or quitting the country. It is probable that a fairly large number sank to villein status, though there is no evidence of an increase in the quantity of villeins; indeed, in the eastern counties they were fewer. At Bergholt in Suffolk (II.287) the sokemen seem to have declined from 210 to 119. The enormous royal manor of Northallerton (299ai) was all waste after King William's harrying of Yorkshire, but it had included 116 sokemen. It has been suggested that in Cambridgeshire sokemen were reduced from 900 to 200, though it is doubtful if the proportion was really so high. There is textual suggestion that some of the sokemen of 1086 did not appear in the record.

'Soke' implies the profits of jurisdiction, the power to summon an offender to the lord's court, if he held one, and not that of the Hundred, pass judgment upon him, and exact and retain a fine, which the possessor of sokeright received also if trial of his man took place in the Hundred-court. The number of persons in the eastern counties said to have possessed sokeright in King Edward's day is large. Sokeright seems to have gone with the land rather than with the man, for we frequently read of a tenant being the man of some magnate, but of someone else having soke over him, and that if the land was sold, sokeright remained as it was. We hear of men who could not sell without the leave of Archbishop Stigand, for 'he had the soke' (Brockdish, II.139). In contrast, Coleman was 'so free that he could go with his soke where he would', yet he remained commended to Wihtgar. Sokeright was divisible between more than one lord, and it could be partial: a man might have soke over his demesne, but not over his villeins

(Wenham, II.425b). Sokeright was a profitable asset: that of Rochford Hundred (II.45b) was worth 100 shillings.

The soke of an entire Hundred might be in a single hand: Ely Abbey had the soke of 5½ Suffolk Hundreds (II.385b), and Bury St. Edmunds of 8½, while of others it was attached to royal manors (II.113b, 127b). But some pleas were normally, but not invariably, reserved to the Crown. These are referred to as the 'six forfeitures', for the crimes of breach of the peace, homicide, breaking into a house, failing to serve in the national levy of armed men, becoming subject to outlawry, and helping an outlaw. Sometimes only three of these are specified.

The enormous complications which could arise from such situations as have been outlined above made the second volume of Domesday Book a somewhat confused and sometimes unintelligible production, often extremely difficult to translate and interpret. Two entries, from Norfolk and Yorkshire, will give some idea of the material: the common statistical details have been omitted.

fol. II.141 Stockton was held by Stigand as a berewick in Earsham of 2 carucates . . . 30 sokemen with 3 carucates . . . and in the same 12 sokemen with 25 acres . . . there belong also to Stockton 10 sokemen with 2½ carucates and 21 sokemen in *Ierpstuna* with 120 acres . . . and 8 free men were added to this manor, and they have 12 acres.

fol. 313a2 In Foston there are 8 carucates for geld and four plough-teams can be there. Morcar had one manor there . . . To this manor belongs this soke: Terrington 1½ carucates, Thornton-le-Clay 2 carucates, Huntington 1 carucate 2 bovates, Flaxton 1½ carucates. Together, 6 carucates 2 bovates for geld, and five plough-teams can be there. They are waste.

Further difficulties are induced by some references to the holding of manors 'with all custom', and to customary tenants. We are never told what these customary obligations are, but we may suppose that they represent labour services and perhaps money dues. For Ely sokemen had to plough, thresh, weed, and reap on the abbey lands, and to provide horses and transport provisions for the monks, just as the radmen of the West had to do. Such services were probably limited to occasional days in the year, and not, as with many villeins and bordars, a regular number every week.

Another obligation was that of penning sheep in the lord's fold so that he might have the advantage of the essential manure. The right to exact this is styled 'foldsoke'.

8

THE TENANTS-IN-CHIEF

IT WAS the essence of King William's land-grants that it should be acknowledged by their recipients that all land was held of the king. In consequence the initial entry in almost every *breve*, and many other entries also, begins with the statement that someone holds some place 'of the king' *de rege*. This is sometimes omitted for the Church lands, but it is made plain that bishops and abbots received their land from him.

After the Conquest, the king was by far the largest landholder in England, while before 1066 there had not been overmuch difference between King Edward's possessions and those of his earls. In only two counties did King William not hold land, the border shires of Shropshire and Cheshire of which he had made Roger of Montgomery and Hugh of Avranches earls so that they could employ their full resources in extending Norman control into Wales. It has been calculated that King William possessed at least 15% of the land, and that his annual revenue therefrom was about 2½ times as great as that of the two next largest landowners, his half-brothers, combined. Though portions of his manors had been illegally acquired by his barons, he had been adding to the royal estates since his original land settlement. He had taken over most of his wife's estates when she died late in 1083, some of the lands formerly in the private ownership of Archbishop Stigand of Canterbury when he was deprived of his archiepiscopate and of the bishopric of Winchester, and, among others, the holdings of Earl Aubrey when he resigned his Northumbrian earldom.

Though his half-brother Odo of Bayeux had been under arrest since 1082, Domesday Book credits the bishop with the vast estates bestowed upon him, which lay in 16 different counties. Robert of Mortain had land in 19, and virtually enjoyed the status of earl in Cornwall, where he had almost all the land which was not the property of the king or of the bishop of Exeter and a few religious houses.

Several personages who were dead or had left England by 1066 appear in the text besides those mentioned earlier. Brian of Penthièvre seems to have been Robert of Mortain's predecessor in Cornwall, and perhaps elsewhere also. Possibly, since he was a Breton, he had been exiled after the revolt of 1075 when 'all the Bretons who attended the bridal at Norwich' (when Earl Ralf of East Anglia married the daughter of William fitzOsbern) 'were ruined' after the collapse of the rebellion this marriage alliance inspired. But there were still many Bretons prominent in 1086, notably Earl Alan of Richmond, Judhael of Totnes, and Alfred of Lincoln. Frederick, brother-in-law to William of Warenne, seems to have been slain during Hereward's campaign in the Fens in 1070-1. Lisois de Moustières was alive in 1069, but in 1086 his lands were Eudes fitzHubert's.

There were occasional influential persons resident in England before the Conquest, e.g. Robert fitzWymarc, sheriff of Essex, and Harold, son of the Earl Ralf of Hereford who was King Edward's nephew. William Malet, half-English by birth, knew the country well before the Conquest. But by 1086 these were dead.

The estates of the Church made up over one-quarter of English land. The great majority lie in the South and West, for the king and his court had been largely concentrated south of the Thames since Wessex became the chief of the English kingdoms over 200 years earlier, and the northern establishments had not enjoyed the volume of lay patronage bestowed upon those of Wessex and Mercia. Moreover, the North and East had suffered acutely from Scandinavian invasions. We have but scant idea how extensive the estates of the bishopric of Durham were, for much of the bishop's fief was not included in Domesday Book. East of the Trent only Peterborough, Ely, and Bury St. Edmunds abbeys, and the bishoprics of London, Lincoln, and Norwich, had really large fiefs.

But some of the southern and west Midland eccesiastical houses had long possessed vast estates. The bishopric of Winchester and its cathedral monks owned over 1,000 plough-teams, and those of Worcester and Exeter were not far behind Winchester in wealth, while the archbishopric of Canterbury was magnificently endowed. Glastonbury Abbey's lands were assessed at over 900 hides, and the foundations at Westminster, with land in 15 shires, and Abingdon, at more than 500 each. A few foreign establishments had been given English land after the Conquest, and Battle Abbey, founded in memory of Hastings fight, adequately endowed. Norman bishops who were among the king's advisers and officials had done well also. Geoffrey, bishop of Coutances, had land in a dozen shires.

About half the land in lay hands was granted to less than a dozen men. The fiefs of Odo of Bayeux and of Geoffrey of Coutances were secular ones, not estates added to their Norman bishoprics. The remaining chief figures are William fitzOsbern, Roger of Montgomery, Hugh of Avranches, Alan of Brittany, William of Warenne, Eustace, count of Boulogne, Richard fitzGilbert, and Geoffrey of Manneville, together with Robert of Mortain and the father of Earl Ralf of East Anglia, who was settled in England before the Conquest. Between these was shared almost one-quarter of England. William fitzOsbern had been made earl of Hereford, Worcester, and Gloucester, and had in addition much of the Isle of Wight and land elsewhere. But his fief had been broken up upon his son Roger's unsuccessful revolt.

A few other men were generously endowed — Roger Bigot, William Malet, Hugh de Grandmesnil, Hugh de Montfort, Ralf of Tosny, Ralf of Mortemer, William of Eu, Walter Giffard, and Robert and Henry of Beaumont. Some of these became the king's sheriffs. The lands of each were scattered over eight shires or more. This was in part accidental, for the men whose lands they were given had held estates which were widely dispersed. Geoffrey of Manneville had succeeded Ansgar the marshal, and Ralf Paynel Merleswegen, who had possessed lands in Yorkshire, Lincolnshire, Gloucestershire, Somerset, Devon, and Cornwall. The system suited the royal policy, which did not desire that any baron, save where military strategy demanded concentration of one man's estates, should attain overwhelming local power.

This, however, was to some extent inevitable. It was necessary that in every shire one man, often its sheriff, should have exceptional influence, and so received extensive estates for his support. The lands of some formed virtual castleries. Henry de Ferrières held much of south Derbyshire and also Staffordshire land which adjoined his castle of Tutbury. Though he held manors in 14 counties, in some he had only one or two holdings. The chief element in the barony of William fitzAnsculf lay around his castle of Dudley in Worcestershire. Baldwin of Meules, brother to Richard fitzGilbert, had an enormous fief in Devon, occupying 11 columns of the Exchequer text, and had recently built his castle of Okehampton. In the same county Judhael of Totnes had a fief which took six columns to inscribe. In Wiltshire Edward of Salisbury, the sheriff, had lands assessed at nearly 200 hides.

Potential danger to the Crown was none the less latent in the facts that men with adjacent fiefs had often been neighbours in Normandy, and might have common interests, and the extent to which baronial families had intermarried. Robert d'Oilly and Roger d'Ivry were sworn brothers in arms. Milo Crispin married a daughter of the former, and the latter was son-in-law to Hugh de Grandmesnil. Ralf of Tosny was brother to Robert of Stafford, the largest landowner in that county, and moreover a relation of Ralf de Limési, and son-in-law to Roger Bigot.

But the *breves* for the individual tenant-in-chief do not always give an altogether fair picture of his local interests. Many of the greatest men of the realm were sub-tenants of their peers, presumably because it paid them to rent the estates in question. Hugh de Port, sheriff of Hampshire, closely associated with Odo of Bayeux, held land in that county of five different barons, in addition to his own extensive estates, and was a sub- or mesne tenant in three other southern shires also, while he was renting two Hampshire royal manors and some estates in Rutland. Roger d'Ivry held Yarnton (155bi) of the bishop of Lincoln, the bishop of Hereford Bampton (155ai) of the bishop of Exeter. The tenants of Glastonbury Abbey in Somerset included powerful West-country barons such as Roger de Courseulles, Serlo de Burcy, and Alfred d'Epaignes, who held large fiefs in the county, but these had often acquired abbey thegnlands against the community's wishes.

The text does not, unfortunately, enable us to identify many of the tenants of the most illustrious men of the realm, for often it gives no more than their Christian name, and several Williams might be sub-tenants in a single shire. But it can be seen that just as a magnate's fief was spread over several shires, so were the lands of his mesne tenants. Oidelard held of Ralf de Mortemer in six

counties, and Saswallo of Henry de Ferrières in four. The extent
of a sub-tenant's lands varied enormously. Some would be granted
a single manor only, others three or four, perhaps in just one shire,
some names recur in their lords' *breves*. Some had as many estates
as those who held direct of the king. Those to whom such grants
were made must have included minor Continental landowners who
had fought in their lord's contingent at Hastings or had followed
him to England to seek improvement in their fortunes. A leading
baron had also to endow his household officials, for a great man
needed his constable or commander of his fighting men, his
chamberlain and steward and the holders of a host of minor posts,
and his knights and trained soldiers, some of whom would be
time-expired and anxious to turn from war to farming. The
chaplain, chamberlain, and cook of Roger Bigot, sheriff of East
Anglia, are all mentioned in Domesday Book.

This lists numerous minor personages with small fiefs or the
single manor only. Many were clerics, technicians, military
experts, foresters, and office-holders. Nigel, a priest who was the
Conqueror's physician, received the quite extensive lands of an
exiled English canon; we find men styled 'the crossbowman' or the
'the engineer' who must have held responsible posts in the royal
army, 'the steersman', 'the fisherman', 'the interpreter', 'the
butler', 'the cook', 'the goldsmith', 'the treasurer'. Some are
known to us by their nicknames: Richard Poignant, the tenant of
Trow Farm mentioned earlier, implies 'the biter'. But what earned
a certain Roger the epithet of 'God save the ladies', or one
Humfrey that of 'golden balls' is a mystery.

Finally, there are the native survivors. Only two held fiefs fit to
be classed with those of foreign barons. Thurkill of Arden, son of
the Warwickshire sheriff, and Colswegen of Lincoln. Judith, the
widow of the executed Earl Waltheof, was the king's niece, and
not a native. Most shires have a section devoted to the 'king's
thegns', comparatively few of whom possessed more than a single
manor in 1086, and we not infrequently find a native as the
sub-tenant of a foreigner, often on a holding he had possessed
before the Conquest. In the appropriate areas many are said to be
foresters or huntsmen, for it would be only natural to retain the
services of those familiar with the ways of the wild beasts. For the
king, who 'loved the tall stags as though he were their father', and

his barons, found their chief sport in the chase, as well as a source of food.

9

THE LAND OF THE MANOR

THE ENGLAND of the 11th century was primarily concerned with agriculture. It was probably no accident that the instructions for the Inquest concerning manorial equipment gave pride of place to the plough-teams of the manor. But other sources of sustenance and profit, some of which were essential to the life of the village and contributed to the value of a manor, had obviously to be included also. The instructions mention only woodland, meadow, pasture, mills, and fisheries, but some reports did not confine themselves to these, especially where a customary due for the use of an amenity was concerned.

Instructions as to how the extents were to be given cannot have been definite or clear. Some were estimated in terms of linear dimensions, using for the most part the league and furlong as units, though roods and perches occasionally appear also. Since the areas concerned cannot have been strictly rectangular, measurements by dimensions could be no more than approximations. Whether the maximum or the average length is given is something we do not know. Nor do we know how many furlongs went to the league. 12 seems the most likely figure, but some entries suggest that a different reckoning was locally in use. Quite frequently only a single measurement is given. Whether this implies length added to breadth, or whether it represents an areal unit, we do not know.

Many of the figures given are in terms of the acre. Here again we cannot be sure that this implied an identical area in every district. We find it used as a measure of dimension, and this may imply a reckoning in terms of the acre's length or breadth, 220 or 22 yards. But other units are used also. The hide, the virgate, the carucate, and the bovate all appear occasionally. So does the arpent, though normally this was reserved for indicating the sizes of vineyards. A great many figures can have been no more than approximations, and round figures were frequently employed. All this makes the mapping of the information somewhat un-satisfactory. It is to be presumed that where a manor contained numerous settlements, each would report its individual quantities. On what principle these were combined to give one set of figures for the whole is a mystery, for one cannot easily add acres to furlongs.

For in some shires we are given what would seem to be the dimensions, inclusive of those of its berewicks and sokelands, of the manor. To what extent they reproduce the truth is in-determinable, especially when we find a collection of holdings said to be 2½ leagues by 2 leagues in size, but including woodland 3 leagues by 1 league (308ai). It is however possible that where pasture goes unmentioned the dimensions may indicate its extent.

The extent of woodland is given by linear measurement, in acres, and, on a few occasions, in terms of the hide. This last was perhaps used as a synonym for 120 acres. But it is also reckoned in several other ways, some extremely uninformative. There is 'as much wood as suffices for the manor' (165bi), 'very little wood' (183bi), 'a great wood' (185b2). We hear of wood 'for making the fences' (38ai), for house-building (192bi), for fuel (202bi), and of particular varieties of wood, e.g. oak (293a2), ash (351b2), and willow (287bi), while several other kinds are mentioned. Occasionally it is classed as a grove (64b2), and frequently as coppice or underwood. Whether *parva silva* implies a small wood or one of immature growth is not disclosed.

It is described also according to its capacity for acting as swine-pasture, or by the rents paid for its use for this purpose, known as pannage. The quantities might refer to the number of swine pastured, or of those given to the lord in lieu of a cash-rent. A large number, e.g. 2,000 (Bishops Hatfield, 135ai), obviously implies the quantity produced or 'fattened', but round figures must be approximations. Swine-rents varied; we find one in three, six, seven, and ten of those driven to the woodland to feed. On some manors it seems that either no due was exacted, or that the wood was unsuitable for pannage; it is 'not pasturable' or 'without pannage'. Some areas described as pasture may well have been woodland pasture. Many a complex manor would have woodland in most or all of its components, and this would vary in quality.

This dispersion of a manor's woodland is stressed in the Kent text. Kentish manors possessed what are styled 'denes', swine-pastures often far distant from the village which gave the manor its name, and often in the Weald, the tract of wild and largely uninhabited country of west Kent, north Sussex, and south Surrey. Documents other than Domesday Book show that this does not mention all of them; apparently the manor of Lenham had 13. They occur occasionally in entries from other shires. Some were certainly inhabited. The woodland of Domesday is that used by the lord and the villagers; we hear very little of the extensive tracts of wild woodland unexploited except for the pursuit and capture of its animal inhabitants, or that which must often have separated settlements from each other.

Some woodland, however, was being reclaimed. Clearing in order to extend the arable or furnish additional pasture, forbidden in places under Forest law, was probably proceeding in many places other than the few Herefordshire examples mentioned in the text as 'assarts'. It may be that in some of the instances in which settlers, *hospites*, are noted, these were engaged in this work in order to found a new settlement. But some destruction of the woodland may have been due to the constant need for timber. Only the record of the eastern counties tells us of differences in the amount of land used as swine-pasture, and here are frequent instances of large falls in the amount of wood or the number of swine pastured, of 80% at Buxton (II.229) and Wisset (II.293).

Occasionally the woodland bears a name. Chute and Melchet Woods in Wiltshire (65a2, 68ai,2) were largely Forest land, and the Oxfordshire Forests are named. The 'wood of the whole shire called *Hereswode*' (230ai) sounds like common pasture for the men of Leicestershire. The 'wood of Fakenham' (II.197b) seems to have lain in the manor of Colkirk.

Swine-farming must have been extensively practised. Even though some of the figures are obviously round-number estimates, those of 'wood for which there are swine' display this. Waltham in Essex (II.15b) had wood for 2,200. Though swineherds (*porcarii*) occur chiefly in the three shires of the South-west, there must have been many more than those mentioned. The dues these paid shows them to have been breeders and farmers rather than herdsmen. Six at Hanley Castle (180b2) rendered 60 pigs each year to their lord for the privilege of pasturing them. Money-rents were also paid; 17 farmers on the huge dispersed manor of Taunton rendered 150s.

The extent of the pastureland is omitted from the record of some counties, and appears but rarely in others, or its existence is indicated only by mention of pasture-dues payable. Its availability was so essential for the maintenance of the livestock that it was perhaps thought that it was unnecessary to record it. In some shires, e.g. Cambridgeshire, it was returned merely as 'pasture for the livestock of the vill', with no dimensions given: obviously it was assumed that sufficient was essential. In Essex and Norfolk it is usually said to be 'for the sheep', and their feeding-ground was often the coastal marshland. Once that for horses appears (Kintbury, 57bi). Some extents are so great that they must represent the sum of those components of a complex manor.

But in what manner these were added together is a mystery. Melksham (65ai) had pasture 7 leagues long by 7 leagues broad; Litton (89bi) 1,000 acres, presumably on the Mendip hills. The Melksham figures must represent woodland in a number of places, much of which formed at a later date the Forest of Melksham. The area of 110 square miles suggested by the dimensions would cover numerous parishes, and is quite incredible.

Some pasture had to be rented by the villagers. At Barton Hartshorne (145ai) the rent was 30 shillings; while from Langford (215b2) six shillings was paid for the pasture, and here there was in addition pasture for 300 sheep. If a value is stated for pasture, this must be the rent demanded. The free men of Fodderstone (II.274) paid a due to their lord 'because they could not do without their pasture'. Rents were also payable in kind; by means of hens at Guiting (167b2), wethers at Hatfield Broad Oak, where ploughing services were also required (II.2), ploughshares at Abington (199b2), and iron at Whitestaunton (91b2). Pasture in more than one place is recorded even for manors consisting of a single settlement, of which one was perhaps downland and the other marshland, for it is said that one 'lies by the river' (Odstock, 73bi). Some pastureland was named (Wemberham, 89bi), or referred to as 'the moor' (Abbots Worthy, 42b). Twice we read of

pastureland becoming ploughland to increase the arable (Patrix-
bourne, 9a2; Swyre, 80b2).

Small pastures, for the use of the lord's beasts, may have been
enclosed. But most of the pasture recorded must have been
outside the village, shared in common by the villagers. The Oxford
citizens shared pasture, still extant as Port Meadow (154a2), and
in Somerset Hemington and Hardington had pasture in common
(88b2, 93ai).

So little pasture is recorded for Lincolnshire that some of the
large areas classed as meadow may really have been pastureland.

There are few references to marsh, for that unsuitable for
sheep-pasture, the cutting of peat for fuel, or fishing, was of scant
value until it had been drained, which Glastonbury Abbey seems
to have been doing in the Somerset lowlands. Yet there must have
been huge tracts of marsh and fen where now we see settlements
and fertile fields, for a map of places named in Domesday Book
shows many empty areas since reclaimed.

But these were not totally unprofitable. For the privilege of
fishing in these inland waters, taking peat, and cutting rushes, the
villagers had to pay dues. Croxton (202ai), for example, had to
furnish 200 eels each year, and Grimsby (347a2) 64 pence for
turbary rights, which might involve cutting peat or pasturing the
beasts.

Moorland again receives scant mention, for its main use was as
common pasture for livestock. The Mendip 'moors' above Wed-
more 'rendered nothing', and an entry for part of what is now
North Wales (269a2) stresses that the land cannot be ploughed, for
it is all moorland and woodland. But profit was derived from some
of the upland. The royal manor of Molland (101ai) took 'the third
animal of the moors' as a pasture-due; that is, every year one beast
in every three pastured became the lord's property. This cannot
have been an isolated instance.

No mention of meadow appears in several counties. It is
commonly given in terms of acres, but in the east Midland circuit
by the number of plough-teams it was capable of feeding. Its
existence was essential for producing the hay required by the
livestock, and it would usually be close to a stream which on
occasion would flood the meadowland and encourage the growth.

Its importance is occasionally stressed. A complaint was made that a weir belonging to Thorney Abbey was harming meadow in several manors (203bi). It must have deprived them of the essential moisture or over-flooded them. Of a number of New Forest manors it is said that all the land is 'in the Forest' except for some few acres of meadow. Though we are not here told of inhabitants or plough-teams, for Forest land seems generally to have been outside the Inquest's scope, there probably were some few men, and perhaps horses required for hunting and riding the Forest, who needed the meadow grass.

Under 40 vineyards are mentioned, and many of these are said to be 'new', which suggests that the newcomers were trying to extend a culture for which the climate was not especially suitable. Fruit-growing must have been so common, and an individual rather than a co-operative pursuit, that the garden at Orchard (84ai) is the only clear instance of its practice.

The extractive industries receive hardly any mention, yet mining and quarrying must have been extensively exploited. We do find references to iron-working and to those who laboured at forging iron, notably at Corby and Gretton in Northamptonshire (219bi), but they are not numerous. Smiths must have been active everywhere, yet only about 70 appear. Normally they must have been included with the villeins or bordars, for theirs would rarely be a whole-time occupation, though the demand for horseshoes and ploughshares and nails, axes, and knives, would be considerable. Most of these appear among notices of dues payable to the owners of manors. The Derbyshire lead-mines are mentioned (273ai), and a heavy due of pure silver in the same county suggests that it was here being extracted from lead, but other sources, e.g. the Mendips, are ignored. Quarries, sometimes said to be producing millstones (25ai, 290bi) are occasionally mentioned. The cartage of stone for the benefit of Evesham Abbey was noted (Offenham, 175b2).

10

OTHER MANORIAL EQUIPMENT

INDUSTRY in 11th-century England was localised. So far as was possible every village had to be self-supporting, at least as regards its essentials. What it could not produce for itself, or buy from itinerant pedlars or in the local urban markets, it had to do without. It grew its own food, it produced its own garments, and it made its own furniture and implements.

Though millers are rarely mentioned, most villages must have had a part-time miller to produce flour from the local crops. Counting the mills mentioned in Domesday Book is not a straightforward business, for fractions of mills appear, but there seem to have been in the region of 6,000. These must mostly have been water-mills. It is probable that a number of mills went unrecorded; only six are noted in the Cornish text. There must have been many more, but whether they were handmills or ignored because they brought the owner of the mill no profit is uncertain.

Some manors possessed a considerable number of mills, which must for the most part have been situated at the components of complex manors, but we are rarely told where they were. Sometimes a mill served more than one village, but division of its produce was not necessarily equal. Ashton Gifford (70b2) had half a mill of which each of two villages called Codford had a quarter (71b2, 72b2). But division went still further. It may be that sometimes an estate had been shared between several heirs, and that each retained an interest in a single mill. Sometimes it seems as if the small farmers of the vill had combined to construct a mill, and shared its produce in proportion to their contribution. We find men with one-fifth, or one-eighth of a mill (Fetcham, 31b2; Tasburgh II.202). At *Langhedana* (II.404b) a man had a fourth share every third year.

For a mill was of considerable value to its owner. Often the lord alone would have had the capital to construct it, and in any case his leave for its installation would be required. Value would to some extent depend on capacity, on the amount of grain milled, and on whether it served one or more villages. Some ground only the lord's produce; they 'served the hall' or 'the court' or were unrented, *sine censu*, or 'ground their own corn'. But there might also be a common mill in the village. Mills might have only a small value, of only a few pence, or bring in quite large sums. It is difficult to determine whether the value ascribed to a mill is separate from that given for the manor as a whole. Sometimes it certainly is, for the value of the mill is greater than that of the manor. Often an exceptionally high value must indicate that the mill was grinding the produce of villages other than that in which it was situated. The manor of Battersea (32a2) was valued at a little over £75; its seven mills furnished a sum of over £42, and since 9s. 8d. occurs in both sums the mill-value seems to be included in the larger figure. The rents and values of mills are often quantities obviously based on a unit of 16 pence.

Mill-rents were often furnished in kind. The most common form was that of eels, for the mill with its weir was the natural site for catching them. We cannot estimate what such revenue may have been worth, but the 300 eels at Swaffham (196a2) would furnish a small household with a dish for a good many days, and here 29s. 8d. had to be paid as well. Salt, swine, and honey are also found as mill-dues. Grain-rents are of fairly frequent occurrence. Sometimes the kind of grain is specified: wheat and rye both occur, and two varieties had to be supplied at Arundel (23ai). Once or twice the medium is malt (Yockleton, 255bi). The miller no doubt took a proportion of the flour he produced, and this and the eels he caught would discharge his rent.

Some mills could not operate where low water in the summer stopped the wheel from turning. These are listed as 'winter mills'. The mill was an important factor in the manorial economy; hence it was reported if it was a novelty, damaged, out of use but capable of being restored, or causing damage.

Both tidal and inland waters made fisheries an essential contribution to the economy. A high proportion of the catches would probably be salted or smoked, and surpluses may have been marketed. We are not told much of sea-fishing, for while no doubt it was extensively exploited, there was no need to mention it unless a manor received dues from its produce. Thus while we occasionally find fishermen and fisheries in coastal manors, e.g. an unspecified number of the former at Lyme Regis (75b2) who paid the Abbotsbury monks 15 shillings, it is of their rents that we most frequently read. Three Suffolk manors on or near the coast, Southwold, Beccles, and Dunwich, received over 150,000 herrings. Southease villeins had to produce 38,500 for Hyde Abbey at Winchester, and pay £4 for their catches of porpoise (17bi).

Eel-renders are most frequently mentioned. The Ely monks got 33,000 from Wisbech in the fenland (192ai), and renders of 20,000 and more are common. A fisherman at Dorchester on the Thames (155ai) owed a due of 750. The Huntingdonshire fisheries belonging to the abbeys of Peterborough, Ramsey, and Thorney were valued at £17. Renders of salmon are occasionally mentioned. At Eaton by Chester (263b2) 1,000 had to be produced. Here more than half the recorded inhabitants were fishermen, and the amount of the due was a substantial portion of the manor's total value. There were more than 60 salmon fisheries attached to the manor of Tidenham (164ai), some in the Severn and some in the Wye, and some were the lord's and some the villeins'. Villeins rented five fisheries at Ruyton (257b2).

Most of the fishing would be by means of weirs and traps and nets, and would not occupy a high proportion of the villagers or their time. The existence of the machinery is occasionally noted in Domesday Book, and so is that of boats for fishing. Fisheries, like mills, were sometimes shared, and disputes regarding rights in them are noted.

Salt was an essential commodity for the preservation of meat and fish, on which depended winter supplies. The minimum number of beasts required to maintain flocks and herds were kept alive during the winter months, for there was insufficient nourishment available for anything much beyond the breeding stock. Though saltpans and saltworks are unmentioned in some counties, e.g. Yorkshire and Somerset, it is unlikely that they were without them.

In the coastal shires salt would be obtained by the evaporation of sea-water. In some places the number of saltpans is so considerable that production of salt must have been the principal industry. At Ower (78a2) no inhabitants are mentioned except 13 saltworkers, and *Rameslie* in Sussex (17a2) had 100 saltpans which must have provided salt for a wide area. We find saltpans mentioned for inland manors also, and many of these must have had the right to manufacture somewhere on the coast. It happens that we know from an alternative source that the saltpans of the inland manor of Honiton (104b2) were at Beer on the coast.

Saltworkers had to pay for the privilege of producing salt; few saltpans are said to be *sine censu*, not paying rent. Rents varied enormously, from only a few pence to the 37s. 8d. yielded by two at Bedhampton (43ai). Occasionally we are told of a rent paid in salt, and to this might be added a due of fish (Hollowcombe, 115bi). The two industries would naturally go together.

There were two major inland salt-producing areas, where the sites of the industry were known as 'wiches', in Cheshire and Worcestershire. The three main places concerned with the industry in the former, Northwich, Middlewich, and Nantwich (268ai,2), were accorded a special section of the Cheshire text. This says nothing of the local population, but mentions a brine-pit and 'boilings', and much about the laws and customs governing manufacture and transport. The industry seems to have been too important and profitable to be left in the hands of minor men. Two-thirds of the revenues had been the king's, and one-third the Mercian earl's. But the Cheshire wiches had been grievously affected, perhaps deliberately so as to inconvenience a rebellious district, by the harrying of the North Country. The rents they now produced were less than one-third of what they had been. Indeed, the area is described as 'waste' except for one salt-pit at Nantwich, but this may imply 'seriously damaged' rather than 'totally ruined'.

The other salt-producing centre was Droitwich (172a2), which seems also to have suffered a decline in its fortunes. Here too king and earl had shared the rents of £76 in roughly the above proportion, but in 1086 the sheriff was receiving only £65 and some salt, while 'waste' is also mentioned here.

A large number of manors in Cheshire and Worcestershire, and in other counties also had salt-pans or 'houses' in the wiches, and some seem to have had a salt-pan within their own territory. This probably supplied its own needs, and some may have produced a surplus. The industry needed much wood for boiling the saline liquid to evaporating point, and there are instances in which manors exchanged wood for salt. Bromsgrove (172a2) despatched 300 cartloads of wood to obtain about 50 shillings' worth of salt.

Honey was of extreme importance, since it provided virtually the sole sweetening substance, while the wax from the hives was in great demand. Thus honey-dues are mentioned in a large number of entries, and beekeepers occasionally. The beehives listed in the texts for the eastern counties must represent only those on the lord's demesne.

A few ferries appear, for a toll could be exacted for their use. But of such tolls we learn very little, though they must have been imposed for the use of wharves and landing-stages, and probably when vessels loaded and unloaded goods also.

The only occasional appearance of certain occupations and amenities, e.g. pottery-making (Bladon, 156ai) or a bakehouse (Cheverton, 52b2) amply demonstrates the extent to which the character and details of a manorial return might vary.

Especially where customary dues are concerned, various units of measurement or weight are mentioned. The sextary was used for both liquids and solids, and possibly 12 sextaries made the *modius*. Two ambers seem to have made the *mitta* of eight bushels, and *mitta* and *summa* may have been the same quantity.

11

FARM ANIMALS

WITH THE EXCEPTION of the plough-oxen, almost all the livestock recorded are those on the demesnes, and these were excluded, except in a very few entries, from the Exchequer text. We are thus dependent on the material of the eastern counties' Domesday, the Exeter Domesday, and the 'Cambridgeshire Inquest' and 'Ely Inquest' for information about the animal element. In consequence, no idea of the total, or exact proportions, of flocks and herds can be determined. The text makes it plain that it records only the lord's beasts, and their quantities seem to have been small in comparison with those of the villagers. There were, for example, only 40 swine on the demesne at Waltham (II.15b), but wood for 2,200 suggests that the villagers had many more, and here the small sokemen farmers had wood for 182 also. The precision of this last figure suggests that this may have been the actual quantity possessed by the sokemen.

The numbers of sheep given greatly exceed those for any other kind of animal. The three eastern counties furnish about 130,000, whereas here swine total almost 100,000 less. The three most south-westerly shires had over 110,000, but the figure for swine is only about 10% of this. The demesne flocks were often very large; at West Walton in the fenland there were 1,300 (II.213). In the eastern counties they were at their most numerous on the coastal marshes and in the dry portions of the fenland, which provided rich grazing. The only reference to their wool is that in two districts at least some of this was the queen's perquisite (30bi, 162b2), and that there was a shearing-house at Stallingborough (340ai).

Pigs come second in point of numbers. Demesne herds were, on the whole, not large, though in the South-west they sometimes numbered 60. We can judge their importance by the large amounts of wood described as their pasture, and by rents of swineherds and others (p. 56).

Only she-goats are recorded, and in number these seem to have been very much fewer than the swine, since they would be kept for their milk rather than their flesh. Demesne flocks rarely exceeded 50, and on the whole were only occasionally substantial ones. They must have been of service also for browsing on and so destroying scrub growth.

Only rarely are cows mentioned as such, but there are nearly as many 'animals' (*animalia*), sometimes said to be 'non-working animals', as there are goats, and these probably represent cows. They were probably kept as breeders of the plough-oxen, and their milk may have been reserved for the lord's household and cheese-making. The villagers would depend principally on the milk of sheep and goats for nourishment and cheese. Rents discharged by the production of cheese are mentioned on only a few occasions, and we hear practically nothing of dairy-farms. Calves appear in a few entries, and a bull in only one (Bodardle, *249b*).

Various kinds of horses are mentioned. 'Rounceys' were pack-animals, and consequently no manor had a really large number of them. Breeding establishments are indicated by mention of 'forest' or 'unbroken' mares (*equae silvaticae, indomitae*), which appear as an exotic entry in Surrey (36ai). Some numbers were considerable: Brendon (*337*) and Lynton (*402*), both in Exmoor, had 104 and 72 respectively. It is to be supposed that many went unmentioned, for there must have been a substantial demand for horses for riding and cartage, while foals are rarely noted. On one occasion a horse for harrowing appears, and even a lame mare. There are occasional references to mules, asses, and donkeys.

The record for the eastern counties often gives the quantities of various animals for dates earlier than 1086 also. But it is only in the Essex section that we obtain a high proportion of useful figures. On the whole, numbers here seem to have increased, for sheep by over 20%. Suspicion is aroused by the frequent use of 'always', *semper*, for it is not very likely that at all material times over a score of years there were exactly 318 sheep and 172 swine on the Writtle demesne (II.5). In Norfolk numbers seem to have remained fairly constant, though everywhere enormous fluctuations were reported. The demesne flock of sheep at Wormingford

(II.66) is said to have increased from six to 200, while at Appleton (II.173b, 256) there had been a decline from 163 to 16, and the Debden swine (II.73b) had decreased from 250 by 56%. But we cannot trust totals, for if we are given a quantity for 1086 where none is recorded for 1066, we cannot be sure that there had been an increase in numbers. Also alterations in the composition of manors, and the inclusion in a manor of the land of free men and sokemen, might produce violent changes in the quantity of demesne animals.

12

CHURCHES

A CHURCH could be a source of profit, and consequently was included in a manorial return even though the instructions do not seem to have demanded that it should be. In many instances it was a lay possession, and the owner drew the revenues while paying the occupant of the benefice a stipend. While there were churches whose priest was of villein status, and who possessed little more than his share in the common fields of the village, there were also churches which were richly endowed.

Churches are mentioned where a priest is not, and the reverse also occurs. Some manors would include a considerable number of churches. Chilcombe (41ai) had nine, but we are not told in which of the villages comprising the manor these lay. Settlements bearing a common name are found with more than one church, and today we often find more than one parish there distinguished by the dedications of the churches, e.g. Fornham in Suffolk (II.357b, 361b, 362), where one of the three churches is named as St. Genevieve's. Unnamed are All Saints and St. Martin's.

In some shires we hear little of churches, e.g. Cornwall and Oxfordshire. There are places whose name-forms include an element indicating 'church' or 'kirk' or 'minster' where no church is recorded, e.g. St. Mary Church (105ai) or Warminster (64b2), which surely had one in 1086. Some churches may not have been mentioned because they had no resident parish priest but were served by a member of a community of clergy who belonged to a local minster. There were, for example 12 canons at Hartland in Devon, and Hartland was a large parish which probably contained several dependent chapels at the time of the Inquest. Only about 175 churches are mentioned in Kent, but documents originating at times not far distant from that of the Inquest show that there must have been over 400. Occasionally the existence of chapels, dependent upon a mother-church, which might easily have gone unrecorded, is noted. Attached to the church of Mottisfont (42a) were six named chapelries.

Churches had been founded not only by kings and prelates and the great men of the realm, but co-operatively by their future parishioners. Edward of Salisbury, sheriff of Wiltshire, had built a 'new church' on his manor of Wilcot (69a2). The free men of Thorney (II.218b) built a church on land they owned because the existing church could not supply all the needs of the parish. Several men might combine to found a church, and the shares each had contributed are given. These fractions are often the same as those in which the village mill was shared, and suggest joint action and provision of land and money to improve a settlement's amenities. A man called Colebern built a church, and if the king would permit him to do so was prepared to endow it with 20 acres and 'sing a Mass and the Psalter every week' for the welfare of the royal soul (II.263b). The small amounts of land we often find credited to East Anglian churches suggest that they represent the glebe land. They are mostly small fractions of the carucate, amounting to ten to 30 acres.

Though rent had to be paid for the church glebe land in many places, a church might also be free of this burden. In East Anglia the glebe is frequently described as 'free land', *libera terra*, and instances of this are not confined to this district. Some such land is said to be held 'in alms', *in elemosina*, but it is doubtful if this implies exemption from all customary obligations. Some church land, it is true, was quit of the responsibility of paying geld, but this privilege was by no means invariable.

But to some churches were attached considerable amounts of land, and the revenues from them were high. Calne church (64b2) was assessed at six hides and was valued at £18. That of Netheravon, which also belonged to Nigel the king's physician (65a2), had a rating of 39 hides and a value of £32 'with its appendages', and these were the profitable manors of Chisenbury and Stratton St. Margaret. None the less, Netheravon church was ruinous, and 'the roof so out of repair that it is almost falling down'. Such well endowed churches had proved a convenient means of rewarding royal officials. Rainbald, who probably filled the post of chancellor, was in possession of seven highly profitable churches, and he may have had several more. Osbern, Osmund, and Maurice were king's men each of whom became a bishop and obtained various wealthy churches.

The owners of such churches could charge heavy rents for their patronage. Bishop Maurice of London was getting 60 shillings for that of North Curry (86b2). Sometimes the amount demanded was unreasonable. For three churches belonging to the bishop of Winchester's manor of Alresford (40ai) there had been received £6 a year, 'but they could not bear it', for they were worth only £4. In some instances it is the parish priest who is renting his church, e.g. at West Wickham (9a2), and he must have hoped to make a profit. It can be shown that where some entries give a value, the sum stated was in fact the rent being charged. Others disclose that churches were being bought and sold. St. Mary's, Huntingdon, changed hands five times within a few years (208ai).

A church's sources of revenue are infrequently mentioned. The principal contribution was the tithe, but we have no means of knowing what this may have represented in produce in any manor. The church at one of the Wallop villages (38bi) received 46 pence from that of the villeins, the chapel at the other 'eight acres of tithe'. But the priest did not necessarily receive the tithes. Those of the royal manor of Basingstoke (43ai) had been given to the abbey of St. Michael's Mount, and Twynham Abbey had all the tithes of the vill and one-third of those of the royal manor of Holdenhurst (44a2). Church-scot is mentioned in a few entries, e.g. at Waddon (79ai), Taunton (87bi), and Pershore (175bi), and in part of Buckinghamshire this took the form of a load of wheat paid by each sokeman who farmed one hide or more, and he was supposed to pay also an acre's produce of grain or fourpence (143b2). The priest would receive also fees for officiating at marriages and burials. When the tenants of property belonging to the bishop of Winchester's vast manor of Taunton (87bi) died, they had to be buried at Taunton, not at the component of the manor in which they had lived, so that the relevant priest should acquire the burial-fees. Some priests had an obligation to sing a number of Masses each week for the salvation of the souls of their patron, e.g. at Heveningham (II.133).

13

THE FORESTS

THOUGH FEW of the most famous English Forests are mentioned by name in the text, there is no doubt that most of them existed in 1086. Sherwood, Epping, and Savernake, for example, are unmentioned, but settlement maps show many empty spaces where these stood, and we have references to land within a Forest without its specific name being given.

The term 'Forest' does not necessarily imply woodland. It is something *foras,* 'outside' normal village life and its agricultural and pastoral activities. Moreover, it was outside the normal administrative system. It was under Forest law, and often it was in the custody of a royal forester and not the sheriff. It seems to have been immune from the payment of geld, and where settlements were permitted to exist it was only sparsely populated. Consequently, with the exception of the New Forest, we do not receive a formal account of any Forest in Domesday Book.

There were many Forests in the country before the Normans came, for hunting was the sport of kings and their entourage. Three thegns held land on the Welsh border 'for keeping the Forest', and Harold Godwineson built a hunting-lodge for King Edward at Portskewett near Chepstow. But under King William the scope of Forest land was enlarged, and those barons permitted to have their own Forest had extended theirs also. There are numerous entries which state that the king has 'taken land into his Forest', or that land has been 'placed in the king's wood' or 'enclosure', or is 'in the Forest by the king's order'. Earl Hugh of Chester put all the woodland of 20 hides in his Forest, 'whereby the manors are much depreciated' (268b2), for swine-pasture and the taking of timber would then be forbidden.

Most references are to the royal Forests, but we are told that the bishop of Worcester could hunt in and derive profit from the

king's Forest of Malvern (Ripple, 173a2), and Gloucester Abbey
had rights of chase in three enclosures (Churcham and Morton,
165bi). Some leading men had enclosed 'parks for wild beasts', e.g.
at Odo of Bayeux's manor of Chart Sutton (8ai). The Forest of
Treville in Herefordshire (181a2) was in the hands of William
fitzNorman, who paid the king £15 for what must have been a
profitable venture.

Foresters and huntsmen, both native and alien, are frequently
mentioned. Two of Earl Hugh of Chester's barons are styled
'huntsmen' (267ai,2), the king's foresters held a small estate in
Groveley Wood in Wiltshire (74a2), and Waleran, a royal huntsman, had a substantial fief in and about the king's Forests,
especially in Hampshire and Wiltshire. It is in this area that we
hear most of native foresters and huntsmen who had been allowed
to keep small estates because of their obvious value through being
familiar with districts which provided not only sport but also
meat, hide, and timber.

About the business of the chase itself we are naturally told
little. It is however frequently mentioned that there are one or
more 'hays', obstacles of the nature of a hedge which controlled
the course taken by driven deer, so that they came within shooting
range, in a manor. The citizens of Hereford had to assist in driving
the deer when the king hunted in the neighbourhood (179ai), and
some places had to find large quantities of loaves for feeding the
hounds. A number of manors had to pay a due in terms of the
hawks used for wild-fowling or of their cash equivalent, which was
often £10, and the sites of hawks' nests are noted, for it was
essential to obtain young birds for training.

The New Forest may not have been the largest of the Forests,
but it was considered to be of so special a character and of such
importance that an unique section of Domesday Book was
devoted to it. This, however, does not include all the land within
it, some of which is described in the feudal *breves* preceding it.

Though it is styled 'New', *nova,* in the text, it was 'new' only in
the sense that the king had considerably enlarged the original
amount of land within the Forest. The misery he caused has,
however, often been exaggerated. The character of the soils ensure
that it could never have been more than sparsely populated and
cultivated. We do indeed read of men who 'used to be there', or of

dwellings 'taken into the Forest' (Holdenhurst, 39bi; Eling, 38b2). The total of apparently displaced men in the six entries specifically mentioning their eviction is only 69, but to these must perhaps be added some from the long list of places said now to be wholly or partially 'in the Forest'. But we cannot be sure that all had been ruined. Some may have been transferred to other manors, which an increase in value or plough-teams in these might suggest, e.g. at Brockenhurst (51b2). On the other hand, the geld accounts (*2b*) tell us that the inhabitants of a two-hide holding in the manor of Downton had fled 'because of the king's Forest'.

There are 46 entries in which it is said that the land is wholly or almost all in the Forest. While the ploughlands are given, no plough-teams are mentioned, and with two exceptions the value is given for an earlier date, as though it now was valueless. Some are said to have small amounts of meadow, and it is improbable that these would have been recorded if there was nothing to use it. In another 57 entries only part of the land is said to be in the Forest. The value of most of these partly afforested manors is given, and is usually appreciably less than that of 1086. Sometimes the value of the portion within the Forest is stated, and on occasion this is the difference between the 1066 and the 1086 values. The logical deduction, since the land within the Forest was rarely valueless, is that a restricted form of occupation of Forest land was for the most part operating, though it may have been the woodland, for which the number of swine it could pasture is often given, which produced the profit. There remain a few settlements in which the Forest is unmentioned, though where the value had decreased the extent of the Forest may have been enlarged. Some Forest manors had land in the Isle of Wight, and if the details given include those of the island portions, these would account for some of the equipment of a manor which was partly in the Forest.

14

WASTE LAND

DOMESDAY BOOK records over 1,300 places as being waste in 1086. But this cannot be anything like the full tale, for often it is said that a manor is partly waste, and here more than one component would probably be affected. Lydbury North (252a2) was a large dispersed manor, rated at 53 hides, of which 32½ were waste. These would not all be in a single place. It is suggestive that many places said to be waste have never been identified. They were insufficiently attractive to settlers to be recolonised, and so their names disappeared from memory and from the map.

Of all the places classed as waste more than 1,000 are within the five northern shires plus Lincolnshire. The high proportion is the result of the deliberate devastation of the North as a reprisal for and insurance against repetition of its recurrent revolts against Norman government. But a vill or a hamlet might become waste from a variety of causes, and these are occasionally specified in Domesday Book. There must have been many more instances of destruction by 'the king's army' than that recorded for Harbury (238b2), especially during the campaign of 1066 which took the Norman forces through at least ten counties before Duke William of Normandy was accepted as king of England. This may not have resulted in much lasting damage, but the considerable falls in value and the deficiency of plough-teams in the area suggest that the effects of the march were widespread and devastating. There are manors which had been raided by pirates from Ireland, ruined by Welsh forays, converted into pastureland, or absorbed into a royal Forest. This last is indicated by entries stating that land was waste 'because of the king's Forest' or 'wood' (Hewelsfield, 167bi; Ellington, 204b2), and phrases such as 'the woodland is useless' (Littleton, 45b2) or 'wanting' (Botley, 46b2), or that the owner 'has no power in his woodland' (Chilworth, 47b2) imply that the Forest had been extended.

Probably there were many settlements said to be waste which we should not think of as being totally deserted and ruined. The statistics of Domesday Book show that many places so described for a time earlier than 1086 were populated, and the land being cultivated, at the time of the Inquest. But this cannot imply that all the men and oxen mentioned had been brought from elsewhere to live on previously empty land. It would mean, for example, that nearly 1,000 men had been introduced into Shropshire holdings once totally deserted.

How devastating the harrying of the North in 1069-70 had been is vividly demonstrated. Just over half the manors in Earl Alan's castlery centred on Richmond (381a2) were waste, but some of the waste here was probably due to Scots raids. Of 61 vills in the neighbourhood of Preston-on-Ribble (301b2) only 16 were inhabited, and even so by only a few people. Of the Staffordshire vills mentioned, 80% were waste. In Cheshire at least 153 holdings had been wasted, and 65 were still waste in 1086. What recovery there had been in the devastated shires was comparatively slight; values are mostly well down on those of King Edward's day, and the ploughlands do not seem to be exploited to anything like their full capacity.

But one theory would have it that the northern waste was not always the result of military oppression. It is considered that infertile upland vills were deliberately cleared of their inhabitants and equipment and that these were transferred to more rewarding lowland settlements which might so be brought nearer the standards they had enjoyed before they had been affected.

The waste of holdings in what is now North Wales may imply only that it had been or now was of no profit to English or Normans, for the Welsh were in occupation of it. Here there often seems to have been no serious shortage of men or beasts, and this seems to deny the existence of waste land. But there is ample evidence in the text for the border shires of the destruction of vills during the Welsh raids of the century.

Quite often land is said to be waste, but a value is given for it. It may be that the figure is the sum to be asked as rent of anyone prepared to exploit it, and we do indeed read of settlers on previously waste land. Butley (264b2, 267a2) was said to be waste, but a few acres had been sown, and a previously ruined settlement was presumably being restored to a cultivated state. In some places men from a neighbouring vill may have begun to farm the land again.

Some effects of wasting were limited. Here and there we find a church, or a mill, which is described as 'waste', and the manors of Corby and Gretton (219bi) were deficient in ironworkings and woodland 'and other things'. Wrangle (367b2) was waste 'through the action of the sea', and the sea had carried away one of the two carucates at which Dunwich (II.311b) had been assessed. It is not impossible that some places had been wasted and in consequence do not appear in Domesday Book at all.

15

THE VALUATIONS OF MANORS

WHAT MIGHT LIE behind the sums given in the text as the value of a manor, or the rent paid for it, is frequently one of the major puzzles of the Domesday texts. As with all other features, there is no consistency in the manner of presentation, nor do we know just which manorial attributes are covered by the figures. As with other items, there are omissions, defects, and obvious errors, and frequent uncertainty as to whether all the assets of a manor are included in the sum given as a valuation or the rent it produced. We have statements as vague as that for Chedworth and Arlington (164ai), where the reeves are said to have 'paid what they would' in 1066, while Thistleton is valued at £3 on fol. 293bi, but ten shillings less on fol. 358bi.

Many entries do not give the value in King Edward's day. It is plain in many instances where it *is* stated that those responsible did not or could not find out what it had been, and gave the same figure as for 1086. Some formulae do not say that the pre-1086 sum is that of 1066, but that the manor was worth so much 'formerly' (*olim*), or when the holder received it (*quando recepit*), and we do not know the dates referred to. The use of 'always', implying no change in value at any time, is invariably open to suspicion that no attempt to record a change was made. Occasionally the time referred to is mentioned, as 'when Abbot Leofweard died' (Ilminster, 91ai) or 'when Queen Edith was alive' (Chewton Mendip, 87a2).

The sums are normally expressed in pounds, shillings, and pence, and occasionally descend to halfpence and farthings. But the mark of gold (£6), the ounce of gold, and the mark of silver (13s. 4d.) also appear, and so does the Danish unit of 16 pence, the *ora*. Integral decimal quantities are common. There were 12 pence to the shilling and 20 shillings to the pound, but the only

actual coin in use was the silver penny, which could be broken
into halves and quarters.

The basis of valuation was probably an estimate of the rent
which could be obtained for the property on the basis of current
population and equipment. There may be instances where the
various rents being received were added together and combined
with the figure determined for the remainder of the amenities,
especially where odd quantities of shillings and pence appear.
Certainly there are many entries in which the actual sum at which
a manor was being rented is stated, shown by the use of 'it is
rendering' (*reddit*) rather than 'it is worth' (*valet*). What we do not
know is whether the sum stated is inclusive of other payments or
valuations in terms of money also mentioned or not. Where
payment in kind was made, e.g. of eels as the rent of a mill, or of
pigs for the privilege of pasturing the village swine (pp. 61, 57),
this presumably was not normally reckoned in the value given for
the manor. But it looks as if sometimes it was, as in the instance of
Eaton mentioned on p. 62. There are entries, too, where it must
be suspected that the value given for mills, etc., is not independent
of that stated for the manor.

How a valuation was determined is uncertain. Normally, one
would expect, the lord's steward or bailiff or reeve would fix the
figure. But we find occasional information showing that the
Hundred- and shire-juries had their say in the matter. Kembrook
(II.343) was valued at £6, but the men of the Hundred said it was
worth only 48 shillings. No return had been made for a Gloucestershire holding (166bi), whereupon the men of the shire
decided it was worth £8. Some valuations were queried during the
Inquest proceedings. The value of Newton Tony (70a2) had been
increased from £10 to £18, but 'the English' (the jury?) said it was
worth only £12. Damerham (66bi), formerly valued at £36, was
rendering £61, but the (Hundred)men put its worth at £45. When,
as not infrequently happens, we are informed that rents are
unreasonably high, it must be supposed that such valuations had
been formally challenged. The free men of Combs (II.291) had
had their obligation increased from £16 to £31; it was stated that
'they cannot suffer it without ruin'. Those who were renting
Pettaugh (II.440b) for 75 shillings had been ruined by a demand
which was excessive, and a reduction to 45 shillings was made.

Rents and the farming of manors shows that manors were being rented, and the practice was probably far more extensive than the text would indicate. Quite often it may have been happening though there is nothing in the wording to suggest it, and certainly we are not often told the lessee's name. While we are sometimes informed that the manor is farmed out, 'at farm' (*ad firmam*), we have no proof that this was not being done also in places where Domesday Book does not mention it. A record known as the 'Domesday of the monks' (*Domesday Monachorum*) of Canterbury shows that many of the archbishop's and monks' manors were at farm. This discloses, too, that the text of Domesday Book may be deceptive. Here Appledore (5a2) is said to be worth £16 17s. 6d., but the Canterbury document shows that this was the sum it was producing though it was worth only £12. From a host of entries it is made plain that rents in excess of just value were being demanded on a large scale, and obviously the lessee, probably by increasing the rents and services of his dependants, or by more efficient administration, hoped to be able to pay such rents and still make a satisfactory profit. That a manor was at farm is not always specifically stated. The text merely says that it is worth so much, but renders a higher sum.

Some of the differences between stated value and rent received are immense. Barham (9b2) was worth £40, but producing £100. East Hoe (45a2) was valued at £3, but was at farm for £14. Here there were only nine recorded inhabitants, a little wood, and an acre of meadow. How such a price could be obtained, unless something is being concealed from us, is a mystery.

In a number of entries not only is the value given, but it is said also that the manor produces an additional sum styled *gersuma*. This term can apply to any form of extraordinary payment, and sometimes it probably denotes a premium paid in consideration of being granted a lease of a manor. It may also represent a payment exacted to compensate for the fact that though the dues from socage land or sokeland remained fixed, the value of land was rising. In a few northern shires a payment known as *tailla* appears. This appears to have been a sum of money additional to rents obtained from both free men and those unfree. The sums are often very large ones, and where they occur they are the equivalent of almost one-third of the totalled values of the relevant manors.

The king had farmed out many of the royal manors. His Devonshire estates, for example, were farmed by at least three barons, including the sheriff. King William probably found it advantageous to be able to rely on payments of large fixed sums rather than to place his property in the hands of stewards who might well cheat him. In Essex royal manors which had been worth £107 in King Edward's day were yielding the king £50 more. His East Anglian manors were farmed or 'in the custody of' several of the most influential local barons, and many passages show how much the financial obligations of the inhabitants had been increased. His Hampshire manors, valued at a little over £350, were producing over £500. It is probably to this practice of farming royal manors that the *Anglo-Saxon Chronicle* is referring when it says that

> 'the king gave his land as dearly for rent as he possibly could; then came some other and bid more than the other had before given; and the king let it to the man who had bidden most of all. And he recked not how very sinfully the reeves got it from poor men, nor how many illegalities they committed.'

It is true that royal manors, among the largest and wealthiest in the realm, must have offered considerable latent possibilities of exploitation. Edward of Salisbury seems to have paid £60 for the privilege of farming the county of Wiltshire. He had yearly, from the profits of his office as sheriff of Wiltshire, 130 porkers, 32 bacon-hogs, varying amounts of wheat, barley, oats, and unreaped corn, 16 shillings' worth of honey, 480 hens, 1,600 eggs, 100 cheeses, 52 lambs, and 240 fleeces (69ai). He had also £80 from the reeveland and its revenue; this implies the difference between his receipts and what he gave to the king. But if the reeves could not produce the authorised farm-rent, Edward had to make up the deficiency from his own estates.

Initially the royal, and other, manors had been saddled with the burden of furnishing so many nights' provisions for the king and his companions and household when they visited the district. These dues in kind had in many places been commuted for payment in coin, which for a large manor, or group of manors, was often in the neighbourhood of £100. Some religious houses, e.g. Ely and Bury St. Edmunds, had organised their manors into groups each of which had to supply the abbey's inhabitants with provisions for one or more weeks, but there are few references in Domesday Book to the system, and then only in Cornwall (121a2) and Worcestershire (173a2, 175a2).

One method of insuring against a loss was refusal to accept payment in coins at their face value, since these might be debased, but to melt them, throw out the bad metal, and then weigh the silver residue. This of course had to correspond with the weight the appropriate number of pennies should have produced, so presumably a greater number had to be provided by the debtor. One entry (Bosham, 16a2) suggests that the wastage of bad metal could be over 20%. Thus we read of payments by the number or 'tale' of coins (*de numero*), in 'white silver' (*de albo argento*), and of coins burnt and weighed (*arsae et pensatae*). These are exceptionally frequent where manors were royal ones.

Another method was accepting counted coin, but requiring 20 pence for every 16 which were due, to compensate for bad money, which is much the same proportion as that of the Bosham entry for melted silver. A considerable number of sums are stated to be 'of 20 pence to the ounce' (*de xx in ora*), or some similar phrase is used. It occurs chiefly in accounts of the royal manors, and refers to the practice of demanding the extra quantity of coins. Rents and valuations in multiples of 16 pence are common, and it may be that the frequent sums which are multiples of 20 pence are based on the payment of 20 pennies for every 16 due.

There is a large element of artificiality about many of the valuation figures, though they may indeed represent the actual sums demanded or obtained. Identical sums appear for groups of Somerset manors which once had furnished a night's farm. Two had to produce £106 0s. 10d., two £100 10s. 9½d. A Hampshire pair of manors, Barton Stacey and Eling (38bi,2) had the sum for which the liability had been commuted raised by one penny short of 1,000 pence; 999 because it was divisible by three, for despite the values given it looks as if Barton Stacey had a liability twice that of Eling's. Several large Yorkshire manors, probably once all royal or an earl's, are said to have been worth £56 in King Edward's day, and others at multiples of £8. This seems to be connected with a figure of 504 which somehow entered into the basis on which the divisions of the shire had been assessed. It may be that these valuations were once equitable, but the manorial details for 1086 suggest that they were now far from reasonable. The Somerset manors which had belonged to the earldom of Wessex paid multiples of an unit of 23 shillings which must have originated in an artificial system of valuation.

Manors given identical values in Domesday Book display amazing variations in their equipment. In a selection of five Wiltshire manors each with a value of £3 in 1086, we find from one to four plough-teams and recorded inhabitants ranging from four to 23 in number. One has no mill reported, four no wood, and one no pasture. These may be accidental omissions, but it is the best populated of these which has only a third share in a mill, no woodland, and only two plough-teams. But such details are not necessarily totally illogical. The character of the soil, the richness of the pasture, and the extent and condition of the livestock may have shown considerable variations. A valuation may have been somewhat arbitrary because rents and services had been increased. The value of one of these manors was double what it had been previously, and the new figure may have been an unjust one.

Other things, too, may have governed the sums stated. One man may have set his price abnormally high, hoping that he could obtain this sum if someone wished to rent the manor. Another might make his return as low as he dared, hoping that any demand from him by the king would be based on his estimate of its worth.

The royal, and other men's revenues, did not depend solely on the proceeds of taxation and the Crown manors and urban property, together with fines for offences against the law. The king received payment, at prices arbitrarily determined, for consenting to the marriage alliances of noble families, for a 'relief' paid by an heir on succeeding to his property, and for administering a minor's estates. Barons had the power to profit by the last two. In addition, the king sold lands and offices at a high price. A considerable number of entries, especially those for royal manors, include sources of revenue which may have been independent of the stated value.

The amounts are not always noted, nor whether they are the price of granting a privilege such as the use of land or equipment reserved for the lord. There are dues of hawks and hounds, of ploughshares, of salt, of honey, of an ox or the cash equivalent of 30 pence, of ewes with their lambs, of iron, of grain, and of loaves for the hounds. Some manors were in receipt of customary payments from other manors, but the reason is not given. When King Gruffydd son of Llewelyn visited the manor of Bistre (269a2) he was given loaves of bread, capons, beer, and butter. In two places 18 ounces of pence had to be paid over when the lady of the manor came there (Eardisland, 179b2; High Ercall, 253b2), and at the first her steward and officers received 10 shillings. Probably similar customs were in force in a good many manors. Income did not altogether depend on what a manor was said to be worth.

Obviously any consideration of the implications of values must then be highly speculative. If the composition of a manor had changed between 1066 and 1086, or the 1086 rentable value given was unduly high, comparisons between pre- and post-Conquest standards would be vitiated. It does look as if often, when two or more manors had been combined into one since the Conquest, that we may be given one figure relating only to the place from which the manor took its name, and another for the enlarged manor of 1086. If this is not so, many substantial increases in value are incredible when the stated equipment of the holding is taken into account. The figures given are at times deceptive, for the copying clerks made mistakes. Milton under Wychwood (161a2) fell in value from 20 shillings in 1066 to 15 shillings later. It is highly improbable that a manor in a Forest area would appreciate to £7 by 1086; the figure should surely have been 7 shillings.

It will be obvious from what has been said above that there are many difficulties to be faced in attempting to compare the manorial valuations of 1066 with those of 1086 and of an intermediate period. For many royal manors no comparison is possible. What is certain is that there was a general steep fall in values after the Conquest throughout the South-east and the east Midlands, which for some shires reached a figure of 40%. Much, but not all, of this can only have been due to the damage caused by the invaders on their march in a great horseshoe from Pevensey to near London, thence to Winchester, and finally through the shires west and north of London. Their routes can be roughly traced by plotting falls in value and deficiencies of plough-teams. But the decline cannot be altogether attributed to this cause. Bad

D

weather, poor harvests, disease, and the flight overseas of many native landowners would also be factors in economic depression. It is clear, also, that the shires concerned in the rebellions against the newcomers which followed the Conquest had suffered acutely. The enormous amount of waste in the shires bordering Wales, in the north Midlands, and in Yorkshire and Lincolnshire, display this most forcibly, and the two last had been affected by Danish invasions. Leicestershire values for a date earlier than 1086 are so low that this county too must have been seriously affected, and a similar picture for Northamptonshire reflects in part the ravages inflicted by the Northumbrian revolt of 1065.

In 1086 few of these shires had recovered the standards of King Edward's day. But in some counties values at the time of the Inquest were considerably higher than they had been in 1086. But this was not necessarily due to increased prosperity. Increases in rents, the letting of manors at more than fair value, and more efficient administration inspired by men who had come to England to benefit themselves, would all push the figures up. Land in Kent seems to have been worth, on the whole, about 30% more than in 1066, and in Warwickshire 25%. Norfolk yields a figure of almost 40%. Signs of recovery from post-Conquest troubles are apparent in the border shires and in the east Midlands. Leicestershire in 1086 was worth almost double what it had been previously. Conditions more stable than those of earlier days may have encouraged a rise in values, but it is unlikely that the peasantry were any better off than they had been in Saxon England, and the small farmer certainly was not. Indeed, a general decline in prosperity is to be presumed.

The king, and anyone else to whom he might grant the privilege, received revenue and goods from a territorial district as distinct from a manor. The information regarding this is far from uniform, and for some shires is omitted altogether. Since the account of a borough usually opens the account of any shire, such details are usually part of this, and since the descriptions of boroughs vary enormously in form and content, so do the extent and character of these payments and liabilities.

We have seen how royal manors could be farmed, and how the sheriff of a county could derive large profit from administering them. Occasionally we read of 'the farm of the shire'. For the sheriff hoped to make a profit from his office, and it might pay the king to take an agreed sum and permit the sheriff to retain what he could collect in excess of this. We may suspect that the additional payments Ivo Taillebois imposed upon three Bedfordshire royal manors were in his interests and not the king's; certainly an ounce of gold from each was 'for the sheriff'. Oxfordshire had to find a three nights' farm; that is, the cash equivalent of sustenance for the king's travelling household for this period. It was fixed at £150. Northamptonshire, a poorer county, also found a three nights' farm, but this was of only £30 by weight, and £42 'at 20 pence to the ounce' for the maintenance of the hounds.

An important source of revenue was the profit from fines exacted for infringements of the laws. It was not offences against morality which interested the authorities, but the fact that the most profitable punishment for their commission was the exaction of a heavy fine. We have seen (p. 46) that the right to receive this had sometimes been granted by the king to a religious body. King Edward gave to his new foundation at Westminster the privilege of retaining the fines of men living on its Worcestershire estates. Some privileges were divided between the king and the earl of the district, sheriffs, or Churchmen, usually in the proportion of two-thirds to the king, and often this was done with the profits of justice. The remaining third is styled the 'third penny'. The royal manor of Puddletown (75ai) had one-third of the profits of justice throughout Dorset, but the remaining fraction is ignored. The monks of Battle Abbey had the king's share in a number of Kentish Hundreds, Earl Edwin of Mercia received the third penny of Warwickshire, and Earl Godwine that of six Hampshire Hundreds. In parts of Kent, where adultery was proved the king had the man's fine, the Archbishop of Canterbury the woman's.

The amount of the penalty to be levied for a variety of crimes is frequently recorded. The offences include murder, assault, housebreaking, rape, adultery, theft, failure to serve in the local military levy or to attend the Hundred-moot, and interference with the king's highway. The amount of fines varied from ten to 50 shillings. Penalties varied with the district, or else some shires set down what others omitted. We have no information about the fines for evading military service in Wiltshire, though we are told that Malmesbury (64b2) had to find 20 shillings for feeding sailors, or send a man from each five-hide unit, and none for Berkshire, where, however, we are told that each hide of assessment had to find 4 shillings for the food and upkeep of each fighting man for two months. But in, for example, Somerset, we hear nothing of national service except that the tenants of the manor of Taunton had to 'go with the army'.

In some shires, but by no means all, we are told of the 'heriot' or relief payable when a man died and his heir wished to succeed him. In Berkshire all a thegn's weapons, a horse with its saddle and one without, and his hawk and his hounds, had to be handed over to the king. In the south Lancashire Hundred of Derby a relief of 40 shillings had to be paid. In the northern shires a relief of £8 was owed by a thegn who had more than six manors, but three marks (40 shillings) if he had six or less.

The fullest account of local customs is that for the largely Welsh district of Archenfield, which was not yet fully absorbed into the Herefordshire of 1086 (179a2). The heriot of a priest was 20 shillings, of a free man his horse and weapons, and of a villein an ox. The theft of sheep merited a two-shilling fine, but of a horse, ox, or a cow 20 shillings. If a king's man was slain the fine was 100 shillings, plus 20 shillings as compensation for the loss of his services; for other persons' men the penalty was 10 shillings. Failure to render a honey-due involved production of five times the quantity owed. Absence without good cause from the shire- or Hundred-moot, or from a military force summoned by the sheriff to enter Wales, cost two shillings or an ox, and these are by no means all the items noted. It is plain that neither king nor baron had only the profits of his land to finance him, and it must be remembered that because we do not hear in some places of these obligations, that does not imply that they did not exist.

Most of the information about a shire's liabilities is included in the description of its leading borough, and it is sometimes difficult to determine whether the payments were purely the borough's responsibility or not. Certainly the profits of justice, 'the pleas of the shire and Hundreds', sometimes appear in the account of a borough. The section concerned with Warwick, for example, says that £145 was rendered between the farm of the royal manors and the pleas of the shire; £23 was paid 'for the custom of the hounds' (to provide their food), 20 shillings for the carriage of loads, £10 for a hawk, 100 shillings to the queen as *gersuma,* 24 shillings for honey, and from the borough six sextaries of honey, worth 90 pence. Of this revenue the count of Mellent, the nearest approach to a local earl, received one-third and 5 shillings. The sums of money suggest that they represent commutation of earlier renders in kind.

16

THE TOWNS

NO INSTRUCTIONS regarding towns appear in the Ely document, and the accounts of the places styled boroughs suggest that only the vaguest idea of what was wanted can have reached the authorities. The descriptions of those within the individual circuit often have similarities, but even for a limited area there is no consistency. Admittedly it would have been difficult to frame a set of queries relating to urban affairs, for boroughs differed enormously in size and character. While the sheriff probably had much to do with them, many people had rights and financial interests therein, and it is doubtful if there was any representative body who could speak for all of them.

No accounts of London òr Winchester appear, possibly because inscription of the Exchequer text was abandoned before they could be dealt with, perhaps because they were so long and complex that they were difficult to condense. Only incidental mention of these, and of Bristol and Tamworth, appears. In all, over 100 boroughs or places with burgesses are recorded.

How to deal with the towns seems to have puzzled the clerks. Some shires had a single borough, the obvious county head-quarters, such as Chester or Huntingdon, and the Exchequer officials decided to place the accounts of these, where possible, at the opening of each county text, before the index of landholders. They caused the four Dorset boroughs to begin the record of the shire. But usually, where there was more than one borough, they felt this was inappropriate. They inscribed the description of Southampton between the fiefs of the Hampshire mainland and the second part of the account of the Isle of Wight. They left space for a Somerset town to head their text, but did not fill it, feeling, perhaps, that neither Bath, where the abbey had interests, nor Taunton, which was the bishop of Winchester's, merited premier place. They began Wiltshire with Malmesbury, but the other boroughs were inscribed among the king's land or that of the nunneries of Wilton and Shaftesbury. There is no consistency of treatment in the eastern counties' draft; Colchester, indeed, concludes the Essex text, and neither Norwich nor Ipswich opens a county record.

Estimation of potential urban populations is beset with many difficulties. Those styled 'burgesses' did not comprise the whole of the inhabitants, and the terms *masura* or *mansio* imply plots of land on which, as at Nottingham, there could be more than one house. Houses, *domus* or *hagae,* frequently appear, and occasionally lesser habitations, tofts and crofts, are mentioned. Many rural manors are said to have properties in towns, and it is concluded that the owners of such manors had one or more houses within them, some of which they rented to tenants, for the renders of such houses are often stated. Sometimes these properties seem to appear both in the account of the borough and also that of the relevant manors, e.g. Edward of Salisbury had three masures or plots of land in Malmesbury (64bi); a house here was attached to his manor of Great Somerford (69bi), and two burgesses were connected with that of North Wraxall (69b2).

There is some reason to suppose that the cities and boroughs were not as well populated as they had been before the Conquest. According to the *Anglo-Saxon Chronicle* 'the largest part of the city of London' was burnt down in the year of the Inquest, and at the same time 'almost every important town in the whole of England was burnt down'. This is probably an exaggerated report, yet it seems, as the *Chronicle* says, to have been a year of 'many misfortunes'. But the population of many towns was less in 1086 than it had been in 1066, and fire is said to have affected both Lincoln and Norwich. The number of dwellings is often reported as less on the grounds that they had been destroyed to make room for the construction of a castle and its environs. At Lincoln 166 had gone, at Norwich 98. Often the decline is mentioned, but a reason is not. There were 344 vacant masures at Ipswich, and 224 at Thetford; over 200 houses at Chester were no longer standing, and in the four Dorset boroughs 334 out of 884 were almost destroyed. York had 540 empty houses and 400 uninhabited. Some of the devastation must have been the result of military action, but at Lincoln 74 dwellings were ruined 'through misfortune, poverty, and fire', and Norwich had suffered from the penalties inflicted on the rebellious Earl Ralf's supporters, fines, the effects of taxation, and the oppression of a royal official. Some men had left the city, and some had gone to Beccles.

So far as can be estimated, the largest cities were those of York, Lincoln, Norwich, and Oxford, which may have had 4-5,000 inhabitants each (Thetford may have had almost as many). But York may have had about 9,000 earlier. In the second rank, with a probable 2,000 inhabitants or more, we find Stamford, Bury St. Edmunds, Colchester, Huntingdon, Nottingham, Leicester, Chester, Wallingford, Canterbury, and Exeter. Smaller than these, with populations of perhaps 350 and more, were places such as Derby, Stafford, Warwick, Guildford, Lewes, Bath, Cambridge, Totnes, and Bodmin. Some of these may have approached the 2,000 mark.

There are also places, mostly in the West country, which appear frequently as royal manors but which are said also to possess some burgesses, places which are now small country towns such as Bedwyn, Milborne Port, Warminster, and Axbridge. It is not impossible that these burgesses were sometimes not resident on the manor in whose account they appear, but were inhabitants of one of the towns in the shire, though none is named in the relevant entries. Equally, where a manor is said to have houses or burgesses in a borough, the persons concerned probably lived and worked in the town mentioned, but the manor received their rents and other payments. There were also places where burgesses are unmentioned, nor is burghal status indicated, except for a note that they furnished the 'third penny' which seems to be a mark of a borough, such as Salisbury, Marlborough, and Frome.

Most boroughs, especially the small ones, must have included a strong rural element. It is common to find, in addition to the burgesses recorded, villeins and bordars, and sometimes sokemen, while the mention of ploughlands and plough-teams, some the burgesses', shows that the towns were not altogether dependent on the products of agriculture from elsewhere. St. Juliana's burgesses at Shrewsbury 'laboured on the land', and some at Tamworth and Steyning 'worked . . . like villeins'. Burgesses 'without the borough', as at Lydford, would spend much of their time working on the land. The Cambridge burgesses had to lend their ploughs to the sheriff nine times a year, thrice as many as before the Conquest. At Nottingham there were six carucates of land, liable for the king's geld, with pasture and coppice, which was shared between 38 burgesses who paid an average of almost 2 shillings each for rents, and possessed 14 plough-teams. Places we should hardly expect to have been boroughs had burgesses, e.g. Tilshead on Salisbury Plain (65ai), which had 66 burgesses and had provided the farm of one night. Perhaps it was a centre for trading in the products of the sheep who must have been numerous on the Plain, wool, skins, and cheese, if the burgesses were really there and not in Salisbury or some other Wiltshire borough.

Some of the burgesses were certainly not prosperous. 'Poor men' appear at Dunwich, and 'poor burgesses' at Ipswich who could contribute no more than one penny each to the city's geld. Pontefract had 'small burgesses' who must have been badly off. What the townsmen did is but rarely recorded; it is only at Bury St. Edmunds that we have a long list of occupations. In addition to priests and nuns there were bakers, ale-brewers, tailors, washer-women, shoemakers, robe-makers, cooks, and porters. But this was a town whose life centred on an influential abbey.

Bury, though it had 'quite poor' free men and almsmen, was one of the towns which had been increasing in size. On land which had been under the plough in King Edward's day, 342 houses had been built. At Lincoln 36 houses and two churches had been built on the waste land given to Colsuen, but these would not compensate for the enormous losses of houses. 'New boroughs' had come into being at Norwich, where 160 'Frenchmen' had settled, Nottingham, and Northampton. At Southampton 65 'Frenchmen' and 31 English had settled since the Conquest. These must be additions to what were already boroughs.

The larger boroughs had administrative divisions. York was composed of seven 'shires', Cambridge of ten wards and Huntingdon of four 'quarters', Stamford of six 'wards', one of which was 'beyond the bridge in Northamptonshire' and is not described. Men lived outside as well as inside the walls of a fortified town, as at Stafford and Canterbury. The king's interests in Thetford lay in Norfolk, but the earl had one-third of the portion which lay 'on the other side of the river', towards Suffolk.

Frequently we are told who owned property in a borough, and

how many houses and what they were worth or paid in dues.
Whether some of these are duplicated by the houses said to be
associated with rural manors is uncertain. Some certainly cannot
be. The most elaborate list is that for Colchester, where most of
those concerned had only one or two houses, but some ten or
more.

It is unlikely that we are told of all the castles then in existence.
Before the Conquest there seem to have been very few. Dover had
a fortification, and foreign friends of King Edward had built
'Richard's Castle' near Orleton in Herefordshire and Ewias Harold
in the same county. Hereford itself had a castle, and there may
have been one at Clavering in Essex. There were walled towns and
defensive earthworks, but true castle-building came in with the
Normans. London owes the Tower to King William's advent, and
as he dealt with rebellion against his rule he had castles con-
structed at sites of strategic importance, e.g. Warwick, Nottingham, York, Lincoln, Huntingdon, and Cambridge. His lines of
communication with the Continent were guarded by Chichester,
Bramber, Arundel, Lewes, Pevensey, and Hastings, and castles
were built to strengthen his frontiers at Wigmore, Clifford,
Shrewsbury, Chester, Richmond, and Newcastle-on-Tyne. Though
in some entries a castle is not actually mentioned, the existence of
a castlery makes it certain that one existed at its headquarters, e.g.
at Pontefract. About 40 castles must owe their origins to the king,
and some of his barons had theirs as the centres of their castleries
— Tickhill, Eye, Dudley, and Tutbury. Baldwin de Meules built a
castle in the borough he created at Okehampton, William de
Mohun that of Dunster in his immense Somerset fief, Robert of
Mortain those at Trematon and Launceston near the Cornwall-
Devon border and Montacute in his Somerset lands.

Only 58 places are said to have had markets, but there must
have been many more than these. It is most unlikely that there
were no markets in Essex, though none is mentioned. Colchester
at least must surely have had one. Some of those recorded were in
comparatively unimportant places. There was one at Melton
Mowbray in Leicestershire, yet there is no mention of a market at
Leicester.

Many of the markets were in towns where there was a castle
also, for its existence offered protection to tradesmen and

travelling merchants. Some places which had markets may have had a castle, though one is not mentioned, e.g. Berkeley (163ai). With the advent of the Normans had come new markets, as at Cirencester (162b2) and Tewkesbury (163b2). All were profitable institutions, for the lord would charge fees for their installation, rents for premises, and a commission on sales. The receipts were apparently divisible, though we are not always told who shared them. Fractions of market-dues occur at, for example, Haverhill (II.428) and Beccles (II.283b, 369b).

The advantages of setting up a market are exemplified by the instance of that at Eye. William Malet 'set up a market in the castle here', held on Saturdays, which ruined the Saturday market at Hoxne (II.379) belonging to the bishop of Thetford. Robert of Mortain's market established near his castle of Trematon ruined the Sunday market of the bishop of Exeter at St. Germans close by (120bi, 121b2); he seems to have appropriated the bishop's market-rights at Methleigh (120bi) and removed the Launceston canons' market into his own manor in which his castle stood (120b2).

There may have been markets also in some places where traders or merchants are mentioned, as at the small Hertfordshire boroughs. Ten merchants are said to have traded before the porch of St. Helen's church at *Bertone* near Abingdon (58bi). Markets are so often found in small towns that we can only think that most places of any importance had a market or fair in 1086.

Another source of urban revenue was the extraction of a fee from moneyers for receiving the dies from which the coinage was struck and for the privilege of coining bulk silver. Fees were high, but the large sums mentioned would be divided between the persons concerned. £75 was obtained from Lincoln, and £20 from Gloucester, but we are not told how many moneyers were involved. Fresh dies had to be obtained each time the design was changed, which was of frequent occurrence. The normal payment seems to have been 20 shillings, but there were variations.

We are not told of all the mints in operation, though the existence of coins of the reign, which shows the place of minting, proves that places such as York and Exeter possessed them. Kings had granted the privilege of having moneyers to their subjects. The bishop of Thetford could have one at Norwich if he wished to do so, while the bishop of Winchester had one at Taunton which rendered 50 shillings, and the bishop of Hereford one out of seven in his see-town. '

Most of the mints were in the boroughs, for these provided maximum security and supervision of a craft which offered large opportunities for fraud. But they had existed before the Conquest, and perhaps still existed, in those small boroughs which had been associated with royal manors, such as Langport and Axbridge. In an age of poor communications, a multiplicity of mints was essential.

It is of the laws and customs obtaining in the boroughs that we hear most, though it would be impossible to construct a comprehensive code from the material. The fullest information comes from Hereford, Shrewsbury, and Chester, and is so essentially similar that it confirms the impression that the three shires of the Welsh border were handled by a single panel of commissioners and clerks.

Chester had 12 'judges' whose duty it was to witness contracts and major sales and state the laws and customs of the town if required to do so; York had four, and there were 'lawmen' at Lincoln, Stamford, and Cambridge, and probably elsewhere also. At Chester, and in other towns, the king received two-thirds, and the earl one-third, of the profits of justice, except when it was the 'king's peace' which was broken, for which the fine was 100 shillings. If it was the earl's official or the king's reeve who ordained peace, the fine was only 40 shillings. The 'king's peace' seems to have been represented by a specified period; at Dover (1ai) it was during the herring season. Not all the following items appear for each city, but they are representative. A sentence of outlawry followed breaking into a man's house and killing him. It cost £4 to kill a man at the week-end or on certain Church Feast days, but only 40 shillings at other times. The shedding of blood cost only ten shillings, but double on the specified holy days. Fines for offences such as house-breaking, robbery, rape, and fornication are also specified. For the last a widow paid twice as much as an unmarried girl did.

Failure to pay house-rent (*gablum*) at the appointed time was met by a fine of ten shillings. If a house became on fire and caused damage to neighbouring dwellings, the owner was mulcted of 'three ounces of pence' and had to compensate his nearest neighbour with two shillings. Ships bringing marten-skins might not sell them until the king's reeve had chosen those he wanted. Those who gave false measure were fined four shillings, and the same fine was exacted for brewing bad ale, with the alternative of suffering the penalty of the ducking-stool. Robbery or theft cost 40 shillings.

At Chester, too, the bishop had certain rights. He had eight shillings if a free man worked on the Church's Feast days, and four shillings from a slave for this offence. He also had four shillings, or two oxen, if a man brought carted goods within his portion of the city.

Some of this information, or similar ordinances, appear also in the accounts of Shrewsbury and Hereford. Customs of this nature, or at least some of them, probably obtained in other cities also, but for the most part we have merely odd items of information. A selection of laws relating to three lathes and the borough of Canterbury, and a list of pre-Conquest landholders possessed of judicial rights in two other lathes, was included in the Kentish text (1a2,bi), together with a notice of those entitled to receive a heriot when their dependants died. Among a miscellaneous collection of ordinances is one freeing certain listed landholders from attending the shire-moot at a place other than Penenden near Maidstone. The account of Lewes (26ai) opens with a sketch of the customs of the borough. Both seller and purchaser of a horse paid a toll to the reeve of one penny, but of half that amount on the sale of an ox. He who shed blood was fined 7s. 4d., while the commission of adultery or rape cost 8s. 4d. (7s. should probably have been 8s.). A moneyer paid 20 shillings when the coinage was changed, and of all these exactions levied for offences, or as tolls, the king had received two-thirds and the earl one-third. There was now no earl, but probably William of Warenne, who had the Rape of Lewes, received his share. Twice we hear that the property-owner concerned obtained the fines, not the king. On the Strand and near the Thames at Southwark (32ai) the owner of sokeright had the fine if a criminal escaped to the land over which he had jurisdiction. So did the owner of a house at Wallingford (56bi) if the shedder of blood escaped there, but not on Saturdays, 'because of the market', when presumably the king's peace was in operation.

Many passages are concerned with military duties. 20 Oxford burgesses discharged the liability for the whole city, but they could pay £20 instead of serving as soldiers. Leicester sent 12 men to serve in the army, but if the expedition was by sea it sent four horses to London to help with transport. Warwick supplied ten burgesses, and four boatswains or £4. Maldon had to supply a horse and a ship; Dover 20 ships, each with a crew of 21 men, for 15 days' service a year. The Hereford burgesses had to accompany the sheriff on expeditions into Wales, under penalty of a 40-shilling fine if they failed to answer his summons. Bodyguards are also mentioned, composed of 12 men at Shrewsbury, and Kentish men guarded the king, some for six days and some for three, at Canterbury and Sandwich. The Shropshire sheriff had to find 24 horsemen to accompany the king until he reached one of his manors in a neighbouring county. The duty of repairing the walls of towns is several times recorded. One man from each hide was summoned to work on the walls and bridge at Chester, and failure to appear cost 40 shillings.

The men of Torksey had to assist the king's officers on their journeys thence by ship to York, and the sheriff of Lincolnshire fed them and the sailors. The Dover burgesses had to find a pilot and his mate for the king's messengers, and threepence in summer and twopence in winter for transport on horseback. Wallingford citizens ran the royal errands with horses or by boat to Reading and three other named places. Those of Nottingham had to attend to the Trent waterway and the York road. Impeding the progress of ships here cost £8.

The heriot of a Shrewsbury burgess was ten shillings, of a Hereford townsman his horse and arms. If he had no horse, the king had ten shillings or his land and house. The Cambridge burgesses gave the sheriff £8, a palfrey, and an armed man's weapons. The toll on the sale of a Lewes house was one penny, payable to the reeve, from both buyer and seller; at Hereford the reeve got the 'third penny', one-third of the price. Here, if a house-owner was too poor to discharge his duties as a citizen, he could place his house in the reeve's charge without payment, but the reeve had to see that it did not remain untenanted, for this would have resulted in a loss of revenue, and the city's precarious position close to an unfriendly Wales demanded a full complement of defenders.

Many of the towns had to supply goods. Warwick furnished 36 sextaries of honey for the king, Norwich a palfrey for the queen, and Leicester 20 shillings for a pack-animal. Warwick had the same liability as Leicester, and also had to find £23 in lieu of an older payment to maintain the royal hounds, and a *gersuma* of 100 shillings, payable to the queen. Among the burdens of Norwich was furnishing a bear and six dogs for baiting it, while Thetford rendered honey and the hides of oxen and goats. Herring-renders have already been mentioned (p. 62), and Gloucester had commuted its obligations to supply honey and iron with which to make nails for the king's ships for a payment of £60 instead of producing these together with the sum of £36.

Miscellaneous items at Hereford include tenpence for a licence to brew ale, the making of 120 horseshoes by the six smiths, who also paid one penny for their forges and threepence for other dues. This acquitted them from further service, for it was they who had to keep the fighting men properly armed and their horses shod. The holder of a masure within the walls paid 7½ pence and fourpence for the hire of horses, did three days' reaping at the royal manor of Marden, and one day's haymaking at the sheriff's direction.

Borough payments had increased since the Conquest. The render from Norwich had become £90 instead of £30, and Wallingford was paying £80 though valued at only £30, while there had been two intermediate increases in valuation. It may be that so much information found its way into Domesday Book, and that it so frequently relates to conditions in King Edward's day, because Norman officials were everywhere trying to increase liabilities and payments.

The boroughs were liable for the payment of geld, though this is not always mentioned, especially where there were only a few burgesses in a royal manor which had never gelded. Cambridge gelded 'for one hundred', Bedford for 'half a hundred', perhaps a reference to the number of hides of assessment, Bath and Shaftesbury for 20 hides each. But Exeter's quota was only a half-mark of silver, payable when London, Winchester, and York gelded, and Buckingham was rated at a single hide. Hertford was assessed at ten hides, but in 1086 did not geld; perhaps it was too impoverished to do so, but save for a single hide belonging to St.

Paul's church Bedford had never been rated. This is a curious statement in view of that which says that Bedford was assessed at half a hundred. Some borough land at Torksey and Grantham was exempt from geld, and the Lincoln account includes a list of defaulters. The English-born burgesses of Shrewsbury made complaint that despite the destruction of houses to make room for the castle, or their occupation by aliens or transference to Earl Roger's new abbey, they had to pay geld 'just as they did in King Edward's day'. If this was of general application, and Cambridge reports a somewhat similar situation, the lot of the native burgesses must often have been far worse than before.

Evidence was supplied to the inquisitors just as it was about the rural manors. There was a claim about two houses and a garden at Hertford, and a dispute over the royal rights at Lincoln. The burgesses testified regarding title to houses, or their liabilities, at Wallingford, Bedford, and Dover, and there was a complaint about a tide-mill at the latter place which disturbed the sea at the entrance to the harbour so that ships were destroyed.

17

AFTER DOMESDAY

WORK on King William's great record of his new possessions seems to have ceased with his final departure from England or his death. One addition was made, but not in the Conqueror's reign, a note of the lands given to the ancestor of the Robert Bruce who became king of Scotland. But the findings of the Inquest became of immediate use. There can be no doubt that many a religious house promptly obtained a copy of Domesday Book so far as it affected their own holdings. There exist three 12th-century copies, not completely identical, of a document based on the accounts of the Ely lands as these appear in the drafts and in Domesday Book, with some additions and corrections, known as the *Inquisitio Eliensis*. It is certain that at some time the abbeys of Abingdon, Bury St. Edmunds, Evesham, Peterborough, and Worcester, as well as St. Augustine's and Christ Church at Canterbury, possessed material whose source can only have been the returns to and proceedings of the Inquest and the information which produced Domesday Book. The Bath Abbey cartulary contains a section which coincides almost exactly with the Exeter Domesday record of its lands. Whatever Bury obtained was supplemented and rearranged, and later copied again; the results survive as her 'Feudal Book'.

Official interest in assessments for taxation remained active even though the unit was changing from the hide and carucate to the knight's fee. A copy of the Herefordshire text was made in 1160-70, and was annotated at different times to show who was then holding the estates listed in Domesday. Surveys for Leicestershire, Lindsey, Northamptonshire, and Worcestershire, giving the names of the landholders and the hidages of their estates, were inscribed at varying times between 1108 and 1129, while one made in Henry I's reign was supplemented during that of Henry II.

Abbreviated copies of Domesday Book were also made, and three survive. They are restricted to the name of the manor, its holder and assessment, and some information about churches and tithes. One at least may have been made fairly soon after its original was inscribed.

Appeals to the evidence of Domesday Book were soon made in legal disputes, one certainly as early as 1108-13. A writ of 1091-6 refers to the record of Domesday Book, and writs ordaining that Domesday Book should be searched to establish the facts survive. Landowners obtained official extracts from the text, and it was used to check the work of local officials. It was referred to daily in the Court of the Exchequer sessions during the reign of Henry II, and accompanied the Exchequer to York and to Lincoln. It was used to furnish lists of the towns so that the levy known as tallage could be organised, and to determine whether manors had formerly been of the Ancient Demesne of the Crown or not. If we possessed the full returns to the Inquest of 1212, an enquiry into who was liable for military service in respect of land tenure, and to the Hundred Rolls of 1274, we should have two records comparable with that of King William's Inquest of 1086.

From the 17th century onwards local historians began to give a transcript of a county text in their compilations, while the aristocracy began using it to try to establish pedigrees. The printing of a transcript which as far as possible should imitate the original by reproducing the contractions and symbols was agreed to by Parliament in 1774. This, which is frequently known as the 'Record Edition', was issued in two volumes in 1783, a volume of indexes was added in 1811, and one for the *Liber Exoniensis* and certain other documents in 1816. Later a photozincographic facsimile edition for each shire was produced.

The local historians' productions, usually an extension of the contracted text, with a translation and not very scientific commentary, had been largely unsatisfactory, and there are certain flaws in Sir Henry Ellis's *General Introduction to Domesday Book* produced to accompany the 'Record' edition. The first really scholarly work came from the Rev. R. W. Eyton, and included reconstructions of the Domesday Hundreds for three counties. Then in 1895 J. H. Round published his *Feudal England,* the opening chapter of which gave historians a novel conception of what lay behind Domesday Book and of its interpretation, including his fundamental theory of the imposition of assessments, which he proved had been allotted to each shire, its quota then divided between its Hundreds, and then further partitioned among the vills of each Hundred. There is much else of great value in this essay, and many of Round's contentions have in large measure remained unsuperseded. In 1897 came F. W. Maitland's *Domesday Book and Beyond,* which, though some of his views have been shown to be challengeable, remains a classic production. Maitland looked both backwards and forwards from the time of Domesday Book, and traced the evolution of the framework of its social and legal information. A commentary on and translation of the Domesday text is a feature of each volume of the *Victoria County History* series which began publication in 1900. The Public Record Office issued in 1954, on the occasion of the rebinding of the manuscripts, a useful introduction to study of the record, and in 1961 V. H. Galbraith, with his *Making of Domesday Book,* corrected some of Round's unsound hypotheses as to the manner in which the authorities dealt with their material. Between 1952 and 1967 *The Domesday Geography of England,* inspired and edited by H. C. Darby, described each of the geographical aspects of the material and mapped the statistics for each county on an uniform plan. A bibliography listing more than 200 books and articles dealing with Domesday Book and published before 1962 appears in my *Introduction to Domesday Book.*

SHORT BIBLIOGRAPHY

(Each section arranged in order of date of publication)

General

Ellis, Sir H. *A General Introduction to Domesday Book* (London, 1816)

Freeman, E. A. *A History of the Norman Conquest,* vol. V (Oxford, 1876)

Round, J. H. *Feudal England* (London, 1895)

Maitland, F. W. *Domesday Book and Beyond* (Cambridge, 1897)

Ballard, A. *The Domesday Boroughs* (Oxford, 1904)

Stenton, F. M. *Anglo-Saxon England* (Oxford, 1942)

Galbraith, V. H. *Studies in the Public Records* (Oxford, 1948)

Darby, H. C. (ed.) *The Domesday Geography of England,* 5 vols. (Cambridge, 1952-67)

(Public Record Office) *Domesday Re-Bound* (London, 1954)

Lennard, R. *Rural England: 1086-1135* (Oxford, 1959)

Finn, R. W. *An Introduction to Domesday Book* (London, 1961)

Galbraith, V. H. *The Making of Domesday Book* (Oxford, 1961)

Documents

Hamilton, N.E.S.A. (ed.) *Inquisitio Comitatus Cantabrigiensis . . . subjicitur Inquisitio Eliensis* (London, 1886)

Garmonsway, G. (ed.) *The Anglo-Saxon Chronicle* (London, 1935)

Douglas, D. C. (ed.) *Domesday Monachorum of Christ Church, Canterbury* (London, 1944)

Sawyer, P. H. (ed.) *Evesham A, a Domesday Text* (Worcester and London, 1960)

Douglas, D. C. & Greenaway, G. W. (ed.) *English Historical Documents,* vol. II, 1042-1189 (London, 1953)

Specialised works

Douglas, D. C. *The Social Structure of Medieval East Anglia* (Oxford, 1927)

Douglas, D. C. *Feudal Documents from the Abbey of Bury St Edmunds* (London, 1932)

Tait, J. *The Medieval English Borough* (Manchester, 1936)

Stenton, D. M. *English Society in the Early Middle Ages* (London, 1951)

Whitelock, D. *The Beginnings of English Society* (London, 1952)

Loyn, H. R. *The Norman Conquest* (London, 1965)

Most of the *Victoria County Histories* include a section devoted to Domesday Book for the shire. An exception is Cheshire, for which there is Tait, J.: *The Domesday Survey of Cheshire* (Manchester, 1916). The indexes to local antiquarian journals frequently furnish a list of relevant articles.

INDEX

NOTE: Names of places which appear only incidentally in the text have been omitted.

Abingdon: 50, 93; Abbey, 99
Acres: 54
Adultery, penalties for committing: 85, 95
AElfgar, Earl of Mercia: 14
Alan, Earl: 23, 49, 75
Ale, penalties for brewing bad: 95
Ale-brewers: 91; licences for, 97
Allodial tenure: 42
Almsmen: 91
Ambers: 64
Anglo-Saxon Chronicle: 1, 2, 12, 20, 23, 80, 89
animalia: 66
Ansgar the Marshal: 50
antecessores: 13, 14, 43
Apiculture: 33; *see also,* Beekeepers; Honey
Archenfield: 39; customs of, 86
Armed services, provision of men for: 43, 86
Army, devastation by: 74-5, 90
Arpents: 54-5
Arrangement of Domesday Book: 17-24
Arundel: 92
Assarts: 56
Assault, penalties for: 85
Asses: 66
Aubrey, Earl: 48
Avranches, Earl Hugh of: 48, 50
Axbridge: 90, 94
Axes, dues of: 59

Bailiffs: 8, 78; *see also,* Reeves
Bakehouses: 6
Bakers: 91
Barons: 48-53
Bath: 88, 90, 97; Abbey, 36; Cartulary of, 99
Battle Abbey: 50, 85
Bayeux, bishop of: *see,* Odo
Bear-baiting: 96
Beaumont, Henry of: 50; Robert of, 50
Beccles: 62, 90, 93
Bedford: 5, 97, 98
Bedwyn: 90
Beekeepers: 64

Berewicks: 8
Bigot, Roger: 50, 51, 52
Boats, fishing: 62
Boatswains, provision of: 96
Bodmin: 90
Bodyguards: 96
'Boilings': 63
Boors: 35
Bordars: 35, 36-7, 38, 90
Boroughs: 86, 88-98; customary dues of, 94-7; decrease in number of dwellings, 89-90; geld of, 97-8; laws and customs of, 94-7; military duties of, 96; 'New', 91; Ploughlands attached to, 90-1
Boscumbe, AElfstan of: 12
bovarii: 36
Bovates: 25, 54
Bramber: 92
Breaches of peace: 46
breves: 18, 22; feudal, 72
Brine-pits: 63
Bristol: 88
Brittany, Alan of: 13, 50
Bromsgrove: 64
Buckingham: 97
Bulls: 66
Burcy, Serlo de: 51
Burgesses: 89, 90-1, 96, 98; 'poor', 91; 'small', 91
buri: 35
Burial-fees: 70
Bury St. Edmunds: 9, 91, 99; Abbey, 46, 49, 80, 99

Caerleon castle: 41
Calves: 66
Cambridge: 5, 90, 91, 92, 94, 96, 97, 98
'Cambridge Inquest': *see Inquisitio Comitatus Cantabrigiensis*
Canterbury: 90, 91, 95, 96; Archbishop of, 3, 13, 34, 49, 85; Christ Church, 99; St. Augustine's Abbey, 99
Carpenters: 33
Carucates: 25, 28, 54, 99
Castleries: 13, 28, 92

Castles: 92
Chapels: 68-9
Chase, the: 40, 41, 71-2
Cheese: 60; renders of, 66, 80
Chepstow castle: 41
Chester: 12, 88, 89, 90, 92, 94, 95, 96; Earl Hugh of, 41, 71, 72
Chichester: 92
Christ Church, Canterbury: 99
Church, estates of: 12, 49-50; exemption from geld, 27, 69
Churches: 68-70; rents of, 69-70
Church-scot: 70
'Circuits': 5
Cirencester: 93
Cities: 88-98; see also, Boroughs
clamores: 22
Clare, Richard fitzGilbert of: 20, 50, 51
Clavering: 92
Clergy, cathedral: 33; see also, Priests
Clifford: 92
Coin, payment in: 80-1
Coinage: 78, 93; see also, Mints
Coins: burnt and weighed 81; debasement of, 81
Colchester: 89, 90, 92
coliberti: 35
Collection of information for Domesday Book: 9-11
Colsuen: 91
Colswegen of Lincoln: 52
Commendation: 16, 42, 44
Commissioners, King's: 9, 10-11, 22
Contractions used in Domesday Book: 18-19
Cooks: 91
Coppice: 55
Corby: 59, 76
Coscets: 36-7
Cottars: 36-7
County Hidage: 25, 28
Courseulles, Roger de: 51
Court: see, Manors
Courts: see, Hundred-moot; Shire-moot
Coutances, bishop of: see, Geoffrey
Cows: 66
Crimes: see under specific crimes
Crispin, Milo: 51
Crofts: 16, 89
cultura terrae: 16
Customs: 86; of boroughs, 94-7

Dairymaids: 41
Danegeld: see, Geld
Danish invasions: 84
Darby, H. C.: 101
Deer: 72
Deficiencies of Domesday Book: 15-16
Demesne: 'Ancient', 100; fiscal, 27-8; manorial, 21, 27-8, 34; livestock of, 65-7
Denes (Kent): 56

Derby: 86, 90
descriptio: 2-3
Divisions: 13
Domesday: abbreviated copies of, 100; Exchequer, 18-21, 31; Exeter, see, Liber Exoniensis; Herefordshire, 99; 'Little', (or vol. II), 21, 46
Domesday Monachorum: 79
dominio: 27
domus: 89
Donkeys: 66
Dover: 92, 96, 98
Downland: 57
Drengs (S. Lancs.): 40
Droitwich: 63
Ducking-stool: 95
Dudley: 51, 92
Dues: burghal, 94-7; customary, 46, 54, 64, 83; market, 93; marriage, 82; wharf, 64
Dunster castle: 92
Dunwich: 62, 76, 91
Durham, bishop of: 49

East Anglia, Earls of: see, Ralf
Edric of Laxfield: 42
Edward the Confessor, King: 13, 85
Edwin, Earl of Mercia: 85
Eel-rents: 39, 58, 61, 62, 78
elemosina, holdings in: 69
Ellis, Sir Henry: 100
Ely: Abbey, 2, 13, 46, 49, 80, 99; Inquest, see, Inquisitio Eliensis
Epaignes, Alfred d': 51
Epping Forest: 71
equae: indomitae, 66; silvaticae, 66
Eu, William of: 50
Eustace, Count of Boulogne: 50
Evesham: Abbey, 59, 99; Abbot of, 13
Evidence given at Inquest: 6, 11, 98
Ewias Harold: 92
Exchequer Domesday: 18-21, 31
Exeter: 17, 90, 93, 97; bishop of, 49, 51, 93; Domesday, see, Liber Exoniensis
Eye: 92, 93
Eyton, Rev. R. W.: 10

Fairs: 93
False-measure, penalties for giving: 95
Farms of one or more nights: 80, 85, 91
Farming of manors: 79-80, 86
Feast-days, penalties for working on: 95
Fees: burial, 70; marriage, 70
Fenland: 58, 65
Ferdings: 25
Ferrières, Henry de: 50, 51
Ferries: 64
Feudal Book of Bury St. Edmunds: 99
Fiefs: 10
Fines: 82, 85, 86, 94-5, 96
Fires: damage caused by in towns, 89; penalties relating to, 94-5

Fish, renders of: 39, 62
Fisheries: 39, 54, 62
Fishermen: 41, 62
Fishing: 33, 58, 61-2; machinery for, 62
FitzAnsculf, William: 51
FitzErchenbald, Rainald: 20
FitzGilbert, Richard: *see,* Clare
FitzHubert, Eudes: 49
FitzNorman, William: 72
FitzOsbern, William: 5, 12, 13, 50
FitzWymarc, Robert: 49
Foals: 66
Foldsoke: 47
Forest: law, 71; New, 6, 8, 59, 71, 72-3
Foresters: 52, 71, 72
Forests: 28, 71-3; value of land in, 73
Forfeitures, the six: 46
Fornication, fines for: 94
francigenae: 44
francus teinus: 44-5
Franklins: 40
Free-men: 38, 43-5, 86
Frome: 90
Fruit-growing: 59
Furlongs: 54

gablum: 94
Galbraith, V. H.: 101
Gardens: 59
Garrisons: 33
'Gatherings': 17
Geld: 23-4, 26-9, 97; exemptions from,
    27-8, 69, 71, 98
Geld-acre (Cornwall): 25
Geoffrey, bishop of Coutances: 50
gersuma: 79, 87, 97
Giffard, Walter: 50
Glastonbury Abbey: 36, 49, 50, 51, 58,
Glebe: 69
Gloucester: 1, 50, 93, 97; Abbey, 72
Goats: 66
Godric the priest: 42
Godwine, Earl: 13, 14, 85
Government officials: 33
Grain-rents: 39, 61, 70, 80, 82
Grandmesnil, Hugh de: 50, 51
Grantham: 98
Gretton: 59, 76
Groves: 55
Gruffydd, King, son of Llewelyn: 83
Guildford: 90
Gytha, Widow of Earl Godwine: 11

hagae: 89
Half-villeins: 39
Hall: *see,* Manor
Harold Godwineson, Earl: 14, 71
Hastings: 92; Battle of, 15, 50, 51, 52
Hawks as dues: 41, 72, 82, 87
Haymaking: 97
Hays: 72

Hens, rents of: 39, 57, 80
Hereford: 38, 50, 72, 92, 94, 95, 96, 97;
    bishop of, 51, 94; Earl Ralf of, 49; Earl
    Roger of, 14, 98
Herefordshire Domesday: 99
Heriots: 82, 86, 96
Herrings, renders of: 62, 97
Hertford: 97
Hide, as unit of assessment: 23, 25, 54, 99
Hides, renders of: 97
Homicide: 46
homines: 33
Honey, renders of: 39, 41, 61, 64, 80, 82
    86, 97
'Honour': 10
Horsemen, provision of for King: 96
Horses: 57, 66
Horseshoes, dues of: 59, 97
hospites: 56
Hounds: dues of, 82; provision of loaves for,
    72, 86-7
Housebreaking, penalties for: 46, 85, 94
Houses in boroughs: 89
Hundred: -Jury, 6, 11, 78; -moot, 6, 45;
    failure to attend, 85, 86
Hundreds: 6, 25-6; profits of pleas of, 86
Hunting: 40, 41, 71-2
Huntingdon: 88, 90, 91, 92
Huntsmen: 52, 72; *see also,* Waleran
Hyde Abbey: 62

Indexes in Domesday Book: 19-20
Industries: 60-4
Inland: 28
Inquisitio Comitatus Cantabrigiensis: 10, 65
Inquisitio Eliensis: 6, 34-5, 44, 65, 88, 99;
    Domesday Book terms of reference in, 2,
    6
invasiones: 22
Invasions, danish: 84
Ipswich: 89, 91
Iron, renders of: 39, 57, 82, 97
Iron-workers: 41, 59
Ivry, Roger d': 51

'Judges': 94
Judith, Countess: 52
Juliana, Saint: 90
Juries: *see,* Hundred-Jury; Shire-Jury
Justice, profits of: 8, 85, 86, 94

King's: Commissioners, 9, 10-11, 22;
    Highway, interference with, 85; Peace,
    94; Thegns, *see,* Thegns
Knights' fee: 99
Knives, dues of: 59

Landholders: 48-53
Language of Domesday Book: 3-4
Lathes (Kent): 6
Launceston: 92, 93

'Lawmen': 94
Laws: of boroughs, 94-7; Forest, 71
Lead-mining: 35, 59
Leagues (as linear measures): 54
Leases: 79
Leets (East Anglia): 26
Leicester: 90, 96, 97
Lewes: 35, 90, 92, 95, 96
Liber Exoniensis: 17-19, 22, 28, 31, 65, 100; summaries, 23
libera terra: 69
liberi homines: *see,* Free-men
Limèsi, Ralf de: 51
Lincoln: 89, 90, 91, 92, 93, 94, 98, 100; Alfred of, 49; bishop of, 11, 51, 49
Linear measurement: 54
Livery: 13
Livestock: 65-7
London: 3, 83, 88, 89, 96, 97; bishop of, 49, *see also,* Maurice; Tower of, 92
'Lowys': 13

Maitland, F. W.: 101
Malbanc, William: 19
Malet, William: 49, 50, 93
Malmesbury: 43, 86, 89; Abbey, 43
Malt, renders of: 61
Malvern, forest of: 72
Manneville, Geoffrey of: 50
Manors: 8-9; 'at farm', 79-80; composition of, 8; dimensions of, 54-5; exemptions from geld, 27, 80, 81; income of, 82-3; urban property attached to, 9, 89, 90; valuations of, 77-87
mansiones: 89
Marches of Wales: 28, 36, 40, 71, 94
Market-dues: 93
Markets: 92-3
Marlborough: 90; Alfred of, 20
Marriage-dues: 82; -fees, 70
Marshland: 57, 58, 65
Marten-skins: 95
masurae: 89
Matilda, Queen: 5
Maurice, bishop of London: 70
Meadow: 54, 58-9
Mellent, Count of: 87
Melton Mowbray: 92
'Men of the vill', evidence of at Inquest: 11
Merchants: 93
Mercia, Earls of: *see,* AElfgar, Edwin
Merleswegen: 50
Meules, Baldwin of: 51, 92
Middlewich: 63
Milborne Port: 90
Military duties: of boroughs, 96; of shires, 85-6
Military service: 43, 86, 96; evasion of, 46, 85-6
milites: 41
Milk: 66

Mill-rents: 61
Millers: 33, 60
Mills: 54, 60-1; tide, 98; winter, 61
Mining: 59; lead, 35, 59
Minsters: 68
Mints: 93-4
Mistakes in Domesday Book: 3, 19, 83
mittae: 64
modii: 64
Mohun, William de: 92
Moneyers: 93, 95
Monks: 33
Monmouth: 41
Montacute Castle: 92, 94
Montfort, Hugh de: 50
Montgomery, Earl Roger of: 48, 50
Moorland: 58
Moots: see, Hundred-moot, Shire-moot
Mortain, Robert of: 12, 48, 49, 50, 92, 93
Mortemer, Ralf of: 50, 51
Moustières, Lisois de: 49
Mules: 66
Murder: 46, 85, 86, 94

Nails, dues of: 59
Nantwich: 63
New Forest: 6, 8, 59, 71, 72-3
Newcastle-on-Tyne: 92
Nicknames of persons recorded in Domesday Book: 41, 52
Northampton: 91
Northumbrian revolt of 1065: 84
Northwich: 63
Norwich: 49, 89, 90, 91, 93, 97; bishop of, 49
Nottingham: 89, 90, 91, 92, 96
Nuns: 33, 91

Occupations: 33-4; *see also, names of specific occupations*
Odo, bishop of Bayeux: 12, 13, 15, 48, 50, 51, 72
Oilly, Robert d': 51
Okehampton: 51, 92
Omissions from Domesday Book: 3, 18-19
orae: 77
Orleton: 92
Outlawry: 46, 94
Oxen: 31-2, 34, 37, 38, 39, 41, 44, 65, 66, 82
Oxford: 58, 90, 96
Oxmen: *see, bovarii*

Palfreys: 96, 97
Pannage: 55
Parage, tenure in: 42
parva silva: 55
Pasture: 54, 55-8; -rents, 39
Paynel, Ralf: 50
Peace, King's: 94
Peat-cutting: 58

Penalties for offences: 85, 94-5; *see also individual offences*
Penenden: 95
Penny, third, of boroughs and shires: 85, 90, 96
Penthièvre, Brian of, 49
Perches: 54
Peterborough: 49; Abbey, 62, 99
Pevensey: 83, 92
Pigs: *see,* Swine
Pilots, provision of: 96
Pleas of hundred or shire, profits of: 86
Plough-teams: 30-2, 34, 41, 54, 90; *see also,* Oxen
Ploughlands: 30-2; attached to boroughs, 90
Ploughshares as renders: 39, 57, 59, 82
Poingnant, Richard: 10, 52
Pontefract: 91, 92
Population: 33, 89-90; decrease of in towns, 89-90
porcarii: 56; *see also,* Swineherds
Porpoises, renders of: 62
Port, Hugh de: 51
Porters: 91
Potters: 41, 64
Priests: 6, 33, 68, 70, 86, 91
Public Record Office, London: 3, 101

Quarrying: 59
'Quarters' in boroughs: 91

Radmen: 40
Ralf, Earl of East Anglia: 14, 49, 50, 90
Ramsey: Abbey, 62; Abbot of, 12
Rape, crime of: 85, 94, 95
Rapes (Sussex): 6
Reading: 96
Reaping: 97
Record Edition of Domesday Book: 100
Redistribution of estates: 12-14
Reeveland: 80
Reeves: 8, 33, 78, 80, 96; evidence of, 6, 11
Reliefs: *see,* Heriots
Renders in kind: *see substances rendered*
Rents: 39, 78-9, 80, 84
Revolts against Norman government: 74, 84
Rhuddlan, Robert of: 41
Richard's Castle: 92
Richmond (Yorks.): 75, 92
Ridings (of Yorks. and Lincs.): 6
Robbery, penalties for: 85, 86, 94, 95
Robemakers: 91
Roods: 54
Rounceys: 66
Round, J. H.: 100, 101
Rushes: 39, 58
rustici: 4
Rye, renders of: 61

St. Augustine's Abbey, Canterbury: 99
St. Clair, Haimo de: 15

St. Michael's Mount, Abbey of: 70
Salisbury: 20, 90, 91; Edward of, 51, 69, 80, 89
Salmon, renders of: 39, 62
Salt: 39, 61, 62-4, 82; renders of, 63
Saltpans: 62-3
Saltworkers: 63
Sandwich: 96
Savernake Forest: 71
Seizin: 13
Sergeants: 40
servi: see, Slaves
servientes: see, Sergeants
Sextaries: 64
Shaftesbury: 89, 97
Shearing-houses: 65
Sheep: 32, 34, 39, 41, 57, 65, 91; -pasture, 58; renders of, 80, 82
Shepherds: 33
Sherrifs: 50-1, 84-5, 88; evidence of at Inquest, 11; responsibility for geld-collection, 26-7
Sherwood Forest: 71
Ships, provision of: 96
Shire: -Jury, 6, 11, 78; -moot, 6; failure to attend, 86
Shires: 5, 26; of city of York, 91; profits of pleas of, 86
Shoemakers: 91
Shrewsbury: 12, 90, 92, 94, 95, 96, 98
Silver: dues of, 59, 93; 'white', 81
Slaves: 34-6, 37; female, 33
Smiths: 16, 33, 59, 97
Soke: 45-6; fold-, 47
Sokeland: 8, 79
Sokemen: 42, 43-6, 65, 90
Sokeright: 16, 21, 45-6
Soldiers, provision of: *see,* Military service
Southampton: 88, 91
Southwark: 95
Stafford: 90, 91; Robert of, 51
Stamford: 90, 91, 94
Stamford Bridge, Battle of: 15
Stewards: 8, 78, 80; evidence of, 11
Steyning: 90
Stigand, Archbishop: 45, 46, 48
Sub-tenants: 41, 51-2
Sulungs (Kent): 25
summae: 64
Summaries: 23
Swine: 32, 34, 39, 55, 56-7, 61, 65-6, 78, 80; pasture, 55-6
Swineherds: 41, 56, 66

tailla: 79
Taillebois, Ivo: 85
Tailors: 91
Tale, payments by: 81
Tallage: 100
Tamworth: 88, 90
Taunton: 57, 70, 86, 88, 94

Tavistock Abbey: 11
Taxes: *see,* Geld
Tenure: allodial, 42; establishment of legality of, 12-14; 'for three lives', 43; *in paragio,* 42; *libere,* 42; *pro manerio,* 42
Terrae Occupatae: 22
Terrae Regis: 48-9
Tewkesbury: 93
Theft, penalties for: 85, 86, 94, 95
Thegnland: 43
Thegns: 40, 86; King's, 52
Thetford: 89, 90, 91, 97; bishop of, 93
Third Penny: 85, 90, 96
Thridings (Yorks. and Lincs.): 6
Thorney Abbey: 59, 62
Thurkill of Arden: 52
Tickhill: 92
Tide-mills: 98
Tilshead: 91
Tithes: 70
Tofts: 89
Tolls: 64, 95, 96
Tonbridge, Richard of: *see,* Clare
Torksey: 96, 98
Tosny, Ralf of: 50, 51
Tostig Godwineson, Earl: 28
Totnes: 90; Judhael of, 49, 51
Towns: 88-98; *see also,* Boroughs
Traders: 92, 93
Trematon: 92, 93
Treville, Forest of: 72
Trial: by battle, 11, 16; by ordeal, 11
Tribal Hidage: 25
Turbary rights: 58
Tutbury: 50, 92
Twynham Abbey: 70

Underwood: 55

Valuations of manors: 77-87; artificial, 81-2; depreciations, 83-4
Victoria County Histories: 101
Vill, men of the: 6; evidence of at Inquest, 11

Villeins: 6, 34, 37-9, 45, 86; evidence at Inquest, 11
Vills: 6-7, 26
Vineyards: 55, 59
Virgates: 25, 54

Waleran (The Huntsman): 72
Wales: 75, 96
Wallingford: 90, 95, 96, 97, 98
Walls, town, repair of: 96
Wapentakes: 6
Wards, in boroughs: 91
Warenne, William of: 49, 50, 95
Warland: 28
Warminster: 68, 90
Warwick: 86, 90, 92, 96, 97
Washerwomen: 91
Wasteland: 45, 46, 63, 74-6; reclamation of, 75-6
Wax: 64
Welsh Borderland: *see,* Marches of Wales
Welshmen: 36, 41
Westminster Abbey: 11, 50, 85
Wethers: 57
Wharf-dues: 64
Wheat, renders of: 61, 70
'White silver': 81
Wiches, salt: 63
Wight, Isle of: 8, 28, 50, 73, 88
Wigmore: 92
Wild-fowling: 72
William the Conqueror, King: *passim*
Wilton nunnery: 10, 11, 89
Winchester: 3, 10, 20, 21, 62, 83, 88, 97; bishop of, 12, 49, 70, 88, 94; Book of, 3
Wood, for evaporation of salt: 64
Woodland: 54, 55-6
Wool: 65
Worcester: 50; Abbey, 99; bishop of, 13, 43, 49, 71

Yokes: 25
York: 89, 90, 91, 92, 93, 94, 96, 97, 100